The Power
Of
HEART LANGUAGE

Seven Proven Ways To Connect, Inspire & Influence

By Monte Taylor, Jr.

www.montetaylor.com

THANK YOU!

Thank you for purchasing this book. I'd be truly grateful if
you'd take a few minutes to REVIEW this book or any of my
books on Amazon—your feedback is always welcome.

To access my free streaming videos and content designed to
help you get full value from this book, please click or go to
the link below to subscribe:

montetaylor.com/heartlanguage

In Memory of Leyland Val Van De Wall

Val Van De Wall was a profoundly gifted spiritual teacher—an intrepid warrior of the heart.

For more than thirty years Val helped raise the consciousness and inspire the spirits of the thousands of people he touched.

Thank you, Val, for encouraging us to laugh, cry, learn, change, and accept in our hearts that through awareness and great love all miracles are possible.

Acknowledgements

I want to thank the people in my life who have brought me joy, encouraged me, loved me, listened to me, and at times forgiven me.

My beautiful wife, Penny—one of the most amazing, joyful, and generous spirits on the planet; everyone should have the pleasure of being in her orbit.

My large-hearted, incredibly funny, and stunningly bright children: Nick Studebaker; Andrea Seiler; Chris Taylor; Eric Taylor; Austin Taylor; Delaney Taylor. Grandchildren: Chase Seiler; Cheyenne Seiler; Brittney Studebaker; Breanna Studebaker; Logan Taylor

My stalwart and delightfully irreverent brothers and sisters: Suzzanne Taylor; Darlene Taylor; Michael Taylor. Our parents: Monte Taylor Sr. and Joanne Bourg who taught us much and loved each of us the very best way they knew how.

My teachers, friends, loved ones and colleagues who inspired or encouraged me greatly, and may not even be fully aware of their positive influence: Jack Canfield; Dr. Joe Vitale; Bob Proctor; Tom and Bethany Alkazin; Dr. Wayne Dyer; Tony Schwartz; Anthony Robbins; Perry Marshall; Larry Weeks; Lisa Broesch-Weeks; Jon Ward; Cathy Piekarski; Jamie Kruse; Charlie and Shellie Rice; Brian and Barbara Remington; James Richard Groves; Karin Boita; Doris Boita; Bruce and Vicki Benge; Becky Groves; Kenny Cowan; Clint Holmes; Kelly Clinton; Fred and Tracy Montilla; Colin and Jennifer Wilson; Bruce Stafford; Becky Brehmer; Arlie Swett;

Mike Sheffield; Garvin DeShazer; Kin Lind; Scott and Faith Hoekstra; Richard and Dorothy Hoekstra; Robert Hoekstra; Marilyn Lahr; Judy Torres; Debbie Murray; Dan and Susan Huntley; Gale Carriere; Eric Seiler; Bobby and Bunky Tate; Kit and Rose Warton; Sam and Nancy DeLeo; Andrea Contestable; Phyllis Contestable; Louis Fusilli; Paula Hanke; Fabio and Lee Okubo; Jessica Mitchell; Margie Tabor; Cindy Tabor; Dr. Daniel Thomas; Sylvia Thomas; Reggie Barbour; Linda Barbour; Sal Piazza; Neicha Hillier; Donald Hodgskin; Joe Nguyen; Karin Santana; Jasmine Nguyen; Steven Nguyen; Dave Hernandez; David Carter; Fred Lockhart; A.J. Siniaho; Paul Marini; Mark Marini; Jim Rombo, Nick Holt; Sam DeMarco; Greg Van Boven; Jim McFarland; Rusty Higgins; Dan Angotti; Bob Piro; Patricia Lally; Tom Orton; Mike Justice; Carolyn Britz Taylor; Helen Brejtfus; Susan Quintana, Dave Perry; Vern McKinney; James Van Duyne; Louis Morton Jr.; Tim Mayer; Helen Mayer; Alex Theis; Bill Cortright; Kay Delk; Rob Grey; Paula Johnston Grey; Kath Kvols.

Special thanks to my talented editor, Sheila Grimes, who holds me accountable and more importantly makes me laugh.

Table of Contents

PREFACE

My father was an 80/20 teacher.

I don't believe he would have described himself that way—nor do I recall him ever using those words. Of course, what I'm referring to is the principle of 80/20 that suggests that eighty percent of our results, rewards, or outcomes results from twenty percent of the causes or efforts we apply.

After thirty plus years of coaching thousands of individuals—when it comes to creating change, and positive results—I've come to believe and accept that only a few things matter the most. The "not as important" things may have *some* impact, but focusing on them is typically not an efficient use of time.

Johann Wolfgang von Goethe stated this concept perfectly: "Things which matter most must never be at the mercy of things that matter least."

In the early part of one summer, right before my senior year of high school, my father asked me if I would be willing to manage one of his service stations over the summer vacation. I was not yet eighteen, and although I'd worked for him in several of his other businesses, I was very nervous about taking on what seemed a tremendous responsibility. I didn't want to disappoint him. Plus, I didn't know how to manage a service station. As an added pressure, his business there on the outskirts of Grand Junction, Colorado, had been declining for several years.

He listened to my concerns and then offered to create a "to do list" of all the important things I would need to know and accomplish. He said he'd review it with me and then I could decide for myself if I wanted the job. A few days later, I was surprised when he handed me a small piece of paper with three bullet points.

"This is what's important," he said, "and if you will agree to these, the job is all yours. I think you can handle these. You'll do fine."

"First, make sure that you open the station every morning it 7:00 AM and close it again at 7:00 PM sharp. Eat your lunch when you have a break but don't close the station for any reason other than an emergency.

"Next, be sure that you enter every sale into the register and count out the customer's change correctly. I'll show you how." (Very few people used credit cards at the time).

"Finally, every day after you close, bring the cash and register receipts to me so I can lock them in the safe." Then he handed me a second and somewhat longer list and said, "Everything else will fall into place. You can learn everything else as you go."

His strategy was to focus only on the essential things he felt were necessary to succeed. And this was, over the years, the approach he used to teach me business accounting, how to improve my horrible handwriting, how to do a basic mechanical service on a car, how to spell, and how to very capably play several musical instruments—all in a relatively short amount of time.

To this day, before I begin any important project, I still believe one of the most important questions I can ask is: "What are the 10 to 20% of the activities that will create 80 to 90% of my results?"

When the idea of writing *The Power of Heart Language* bubbled to the surface of my thoughts several years ago, I recognized there was already a vast library of existing material related to the science of improving human relationships. I decided that for my book project, I would focus squarely on the highest-leverage skills: those with the greatest possible impact on the quality and richness of human interconnection.

I found my answer by first formulating the right question: Assuming anyone is committed to building richer, deeper, and more meaningful relationships with others, then what are the most important qualities, attributes, skills, people communications or language habits that would create 80 to 90% of his or her results?

Of course, there are many dozens of relationship-building skills from which to choose. But I firmly believe these are the most significant. My list is very concise and includes only seven developable, principle-based "people-communication" abilities. In my experience, these seven "heart language skills" offer each of us the most straightforward pathway to deepening our connection to the world and to the people we care about.

If you commit to practicing and improving your "heart-habitudes", I believe you can begin an immensely gratifying journey that will awaken your spirit, and at the same time inspire the hearts, minds, and perhaps even the very souls of everyone you touch.

INTRODUCTION

What Is A Habitude?

Sit down before a fact as a little child, and be prepared to give up every preconceived notion, follow humbly wherever and to whatever abyss Nature leads, or you shall learn nothing.
— T. H. Huxley

After freely admitting in advance that I have a particular answer in my mind, one of my favorite questions in a coaching session or a workshop is to ask people to respond to this: "If you had to choose a single ability—the one that in your opinion offered you the greatest capacity to influence others, and to help you succeed personally—what skill would you choose?"

After a brief pause, some of the more common responses are leadership, public speaking, and some version of 'people persuasion'. It's not surprising that participants will suggest salesmanship, resilience, hard work, dedication, and persistence.

Some will propose, "Just love others." (I especially appreciate this response because it suggests the idea that love might be a 'people skill' and not simply an emotion or feeling.)

It's rare for anyone to identify the skill that I have in mind, so I will continue by offering another hint or two:

"Everyone has heard of this. And, not having this particular talent or skill suggests a significant personal character deficiency. In fact, cultural anthropologists report the absence of it is universally despised by almost every civilization and religion."

My added clues tease out new responses such as honesty, integrity, and faithfulness, but still not the skill I'm looking for.

After a few more tries, if no one proposes it, I will ask, "Would you be willing to consider the possibility that one of the most powerful, people-pleasing, influential, yet underused life success skills, is the willingness and ability to regularly express gratitude?"

Would you?

What makes my, "Guess which skill I'm thinking of?" exercise more challenging is that most of us don't think of gratitude as a people skill. Instead, we would call it an attitude or emotion. We don't often think of gratitude as in important life skill one can develop with practice.

Most people consider gratitude to be a feeling—meaning that it is either felt or not—and similar to the action of a light switch, it is either on off, with nothing in between.

We can all agree that there's always room for a little more thankfulness in life, but could gratitude hold more power or offer even more benefits to our lives than we realize? Could gratitude be a critical success principle?

Beyond the hundreds of inspirational quotes about gratitude, what proof is there that a profound expression of appreciation to others, makes any substantial difference in human performance or relationships?

Assuming that it's possible to practice and develop even more gratitude, why should a person consider it? Is more gratitude worthwhile? Can it bring us more happiness? Financial success? Improved health? Better relationships?

These are among the questions I will explore in *The Power of Heart Language*. And I believe some of the answers are frankly astonishing.

I began to think about gratitude as a coachable skill, or a "habitude", in part from my experiences many years ago as a personal manager and producer in the entertainment industry. My father was an exceptional big-band-style musician, and although I was inspired to follow suit, I chose rock and pop music. I was fortunate to evolve as a professional musician and bandleader and enjoyed an exciting career. I also had the delightful opportunity to meet and work with many exceptional musicians and entertainers.

Gradually I was drawn more to the producing and directing aspects of the music business and eventually abandoned my musical career to launch a management company. For nearly two decades I focused on guiding the careers of other musicians, singers, and performing artists.

Over time I noticed how much easier and more productive it was to manage clients who expressed a genuine sense of gratitude. It was a massive bonus when an entertainer's "thankful spirit" was evident in both their on and off-stage practices. It became apparent that those who were sincerely grateful for the chance to share their artistry, not only had the greatest emotional impact on their audience, but also seemed to regularly attract the best career opportunities.

On the other hand, I encountered (and observed) entertainers who still somehow managed to stumble and fail regardless of their extraordinary talents. One of the reasons for their failure was an attitude of entitlement and thanklessness.

I've had the opportunity to discuss my unscientific observation with other agents and managers from both the music and the sports industries. Many have agreed that beyond sheer talent, the one attribute that's worth pure gold to career success and longevity, is the client with a grateful attitude.

The iconic, "help me help you" and "show me the money" scenes from the delightful movie, *Jerry Maguire*, comically, yet profoundly, underscore how entitlement and cynicism kept Jerry's client from gaining the endorsements, recognition, and contract he craved. The breakthrough came only after the star running back (played by the brilliant Cuba Gooding Jr.) rediscovered his youthful appreciation and gratitude for the game he loved.

Years ago, on one of my many business trips to Las Vegas, a friend was the opening act comedian for Loretta Lynn. Following their first night together, my friend offered to introduce me to Loretta. Somehow our social call lasted more than an hour, visiting and sitting cross-legged with Loretta on her dressing room floor laughing and sharing show-biz stories.

I'd worked with many stars, so I wasn't star-struck, but I was smitten with her down-home, humble demeanor and gratitude. She was thankful the casino hotel hired her, grateful for the challenge and the people who supported her, and openly appreciative that we took the time to visit with her. I left with the strong sense that gratitude played no small part in Loretta Lynn's long and fruitful career.

In 1973, my great friend and colleague, singer-songwriter Clint Holmes, experienced his first and only hit recording, *Playgrounds In My Mind*. While Clint is an extraordinary singer-performer, with an international hit that initially launched his career, in my opinion it is Clint's continuing humility and gratitude—combined with his talent—that have sustained his very successful career for more than four decades.

Eventually, I left the entertainment industry to begin mentoring and coaching executives and entrepreneurs. Again, I continued to notice that clients who were less defensive, coachable, open to learning, and grateful for the good and the not-so-good experiences, were much more successful at achieving their goals and attracting others willing to help them realize their ambitions.

Coaching and mentoring is a valuable learning opportunity; it's an experience that can heighten your understanding of what motivates people and what keeps people stuck. Importantly, I discovered also that if you want to coach, you must also be *willing* to be coached—because either one alone can leave you empty. So I opened myself to the experience of being coached by others.

One of the most gifted individuals I had the pleasure of knowing, and being mentored by, was Leyland Val Van De Wall. Val was an author and spiritual teacher who traveled the world for over thirty years speaking and changing people's lives with his two-day personal effectiveness workshops, appropriately titled, "Habitudes."

People loved Val for his unique style, his delightful sense of humor, and his astonishing ability to first "read," and then redirect people's belief systems. Any of his past students would likely recall this proclamation from Val, "Let us not look backward in anger, or forward in fear, but around in awareness." (A quote by James Thurber.)

Val stressed the importance of elevating one's consciousness by accessing greater levels of awareness, "letting go of anger from the past, and moving forward through the fear of change or fear of the future." He taught thousands of his students to understand that these were foundational keys to success, achievement, better relationships and true happiness!

I recall one student challenging him. "So are you saying awareness is the most important thing we should work on?" Val thought a moment and responded, "No. It's the second-most important."

Of course, the rest of us immediately wanted to know what Val believed was *MOST* important

Employing his "here's a great learning moment" style of teaching, Val paused, waiting until he had everyone's complete attention. Then he offered this: "What all human beings need to work on—to evolve spiritually—is gratitude."

"Gratitude has a unique vibration," he claimed. "Gratitude invokes the positive law of attraction, and ingratitude invokes the law of repulsion. So work on your thankfulness. Figure out how to be genuinely grateful for everything that happens to you. Find the good parts. See the lesson. Be thankful for every person and every event or circumstance that you attract into your life—willingly or unwillingly—no matter how painful it may seem to you at the time."

Val believed that once you convert awareness into positive intention, it becomes an ingrained habit, and your resulting *habitude* will begin to manifest miracles in your physical life.

And, the great Roman orator and statesman, Cicero, must have agreed for he called gratitude, "Not only the greatest of all virtues—but the parent of all others."

There is a tremendous amount of information available today on the principles of success and achievement. However, *The Power of Heart Language*, by design, has a narrow focus. It is about rediscovering seven compelling, powerful, and time-honored principles of human connection. Essential to each of these principles is the ability to embrace and express empathy—because empathy is fundamental to all successful relationships.

In its essence, "heart language" is a metaphor for the idea of learning how to communicate with a spoken (and unspoken) vocabulary of empathy that naturally resonates with others.

Although at times I'll reference studies and newly emerging science that supports these seven heart language habitudes, I'm not claiming these are newly discovered principles. Instead, my overarching emphasis is to reintroduce and inspire you to *"pay much greater attention"* to a few proven and time-honored themes of communication— seven "habitudes" that can bring unexpected blessings into your life, and into the lives of people you touch.

The idea of "paying attention" brings to mind one of the evocative lyrics from the beautiful song, *God Bless The Child*, written in 1939 by Billie Holiday and Arthur Herzog:

"Them that's got shall have."
"Them that's not shall lose."
"So the Bible says, and it still is news."

To me, an interesting "life clue" springs from the 3rd line:

"So the Bible says, and it still is news."

I believe the lyric suggests that sometimes the most important things in life are right there in front of our nose—accessible; unhidden; unconcealed; and like ancient or biblical truths, they have always been available to use to our advantage, or to guide us. But, *we must pay attention*. These profound truths and principles are *not* news—but like it or not—still news to *some*.

To allay my fears that perhaps, despite my best efforts, the reader might still miss the essential message of *The Power of Heart Language*, I'm going to do my very best to describe and summarize the message in advance.

> There is an undeniable and compelling 'heart language' that has a powerfully positive effect on human connection. It is not vague, mysterious, or even difficult to understand. But to speak this language fluently requires a small amount of consistent discipline and the willingness to change a few deeply rooted habits.
>
> This heart language resonates and *speaks* to both the conscious and non-conscious parts in each of us; its effects and benefits are multi-directional—so that as you affect others, you also affect yourself. The immense power of heart language—and its ability to transform and empower—is available to anyone who is willing to cultivate and practice it.
>
> Heart language consists of seven extraordinary people communication skills—seven habitudes: Sharing Gratitude, Embracing Forgiveness, Listening Fearlessly, Spreading Encouragement, Leaking Joy, Nurturing Vulnerability, and Avoiding Judgment.

From the very moment you begin to develop your heart language skills, you will attract more connectedness, more peace, more joy, and experience more *positive* influence over people. You will feel the confidence that comes with your ability to communicate more directly to the hearts and minds—and perhaps the very souls of others.

And so, as we begin in Chapter One, you'll discover the astonishing power of the very first language of the heart: Sharing Gratitude!

I won't pretend that I have perfected these seven skills; I'm still working continually to nurture and develop them myself. Nor do I have the desire to create a new definition of love. Authors, poets, and philosophers, who are much more gifted than I, have been trying to do so for thousands of years.

For the purpose of *The Power of Heart Language*, I'd like to respectfully borrow Dr. Scott Peck's definition of love, from his brilliant work, *The Road Less Traveled*. Peck defined true love this way:

> Love is the *will* to extend oneself for the purpose of nurturing one's own, or another's spiritual growth. Genuine love is volitional (meaning a choice) rather than emotional. The person who truly loves *does so because of a decision to love*; they've made a commitment to be loving—whether or not the feeling is handy at any given moment.

Yes, we are all human. And like it or not, there will be moments in your relationships, however brief, when "You've lost that loving feeling."

Sharing Gratitude, Embracing Forgiveness, Listening Fearlessly, Spreading Encouragement, Leaking Joy, Nurturing Vulnerability, and Avoiding Judgment are skills that add up to real love. And as Peck suggested in his definition of love, they are volitional; they require the will to do so. Therefore, if you're *willing* to read on and temporarily suspend what you think you already know about these seven skills, then please join me and read on.

I firmly believe sharpening your "heart language skills" will weave a marvelous tapestry of possibilities for deeper connections, richer and more satisfying relationships, improved well-being, and greater success in all endeavors that benefit from better communications with others.

Beyond introducing the seven heart language habitudes and their fascinating benefits, every chapter will end with actionable ideas and exercises to help *"inspire your will"* and to encourage you.

If you are willing to commit to practicing and improving even one of these skills (Hint: consider Sharing Gratitude first), I believe your life will begin to change positively—perhaps even more quickly than you imagined—and in ways you may not have dreamed were possible.

CHAPTER ONE

The Habitude of Sharing Gratitude

The mind is where knowledge resides, and the heart is where wisdom resides.
—Tony Schwartz

The First Language of The Heart

Ask people to describe the character traits they want most from their spouse, close friends or significant other, and these qualities are (typically) what you'll hear: loving; understanding; supportive; emotionally available; a sense of humor; always-there-for-me; positive; upbeat; faithfulness, and so on.

It's interesting that gratefulness or thankfulness almost never appear on anyone's list of, "the things I need and want most from my friends, spouse or lover."

Gratitude, like personal hygiene, is not something we pay much attention to until it's conspicuously absent in others. We tend not to notice it until we experience a relationship without it, and suffer the emptiness of ingratitude. No pun intended—we take gratitude for granted—until it's severely lacking.

Most of us, when we were young, were reminded by our parents or teachers to be grateful. Beyond learning to say 'please' and 'thank you', we've also been given examples in our literature to live in appreciation of life's gifts ... to be grateful for those have been good to us ... and of course, avoid being ungrateful!

Across time, ingratitude has been treated as a vice. Perhaps it's not surprising that most people and most cultures universally despise ungratefulness. The great German philosopher, Immanuel Kant, called ingratitude, "the essence of vileness." James Thomson wrote, "Ingratitude is treason to mankind." David Hume claimed that ingratitude is, "the most horrible and unnatural crime a person is capable of committing."

These are strong statements, but to help get you in the mood, imagine for a moment that you choose to hold the door open for someone struggling physically. Then for the next several minutes, you are held hostage as that person, their entire family plus several stragglers, quickly dash through. Everyone proceeds as if you were the appointed door person. And adding insult to injury, everyone's in too much of a hurry to offer a simple 'thank you' or a smile in appreciation.

We've all had similar experiences, and most of us can share stories about people who failed to offer expressions of thanks. Of course, you didn't hold the door open because you needed some reward or acknowledgment. You were courteous. But absent a little appreciation, how did the thanklessness make you feel? Care to open the door for the thoughtless horde the next time around?

To most human beings, ingratitude is an annoying sharp fingernail scratching on the psychic chalkboard of the soul. For any of us on the receiving end of ingratitude, it is tough to ignore. Take a deep breath. Unless you're a saint, it's easy to get cynical.

To fully understand the positive power and influence of gratitude, it is important also to understand the destructive consequences that arise from its polar opposite: ingratitude. The chronically ungrateful become emotional and economic victims of their thanklessness. Ingratitude damages relationships and tends to foster depression and disease, destroy productivity, and diminishes the joy of life.

On the other hand, the expression of pure gratitude encourages and promotes positive change, nurtures relationships, elevates our moods and energy, improves our physical and mental health, heightens our productivity, and enriches our lives in dozens of unexpected ways.

If there were a contest to recognize and crown the highest and best language of the heart, I would nominate and elect the enchanting and spiritual phenomenon known as gratitude.

The Science of Gratitude

The word gratitude stems from the Latin, "gratia", meaning grateful, and pertains to kindness and the beauty of giving and receiving. And according to one study, gratitude is "the most common, distinct positive emotional affect experienced by 90% of all adults." (Chipperfield, Perry & Weiner, 2004)

As a social behavior, gratitude has widespread and timeless appeal across the vast majority of cultures, including the Christian, Muslim, Jewish and Hindu traditions. In all cultures, the "spirit of gratitude" is typically associated with a high satisfaction of life, optimal functioning, and universal wellbeing. (Dumas, Johnson & Lynch, 2002)

We see gratitude as the recognition of the gifts in one's life, but is gratitude a social concept, social behavior, emotion, a chosen attitude, a virtue or a people skill? Perhaps it is all of these. Perhaps it is much more!

A variety of clinical trials report that the practice of gratitude can have a dramatic and lasting impact on a person's life. Gratitude has been shown to lower blood pressure, improve immune function, promote happiness and well-being, and spur continued acts of helpfulness, generosity, and cooperation. (Emmons and McCullough 2003)

Emerging research demonstrates that gratitude enhances nearly all aspects of the human experience and creates tangible benefits that many may find quite surprising—if not astonishing.

Neurochemical research is beginning to shed some light on what goes on in your brain when you appreciate (and acknowledge) that something good that has happened to you. It appears that hormones circulating in the blood and nerve transmitters in the brain may be the biochemical correlates of gratitude.

For example, we know that dopamine and serotonin circulating in some parts of the brain are related to happiness and other pleasurable feelings. For reasons not entirely understood at this time, a sense of gratitude and appreciation appear to be linked to increased production of these "happy hormones" in the brain. We don't know for sure whether these linkages are correlational or causal, or if gratitude turns on dopamine or ingratitude turns dopamine off.

However, what we do know is that *the act and the practice of affirming the goodness in one's life* and, *recognizing the source of this goodness*, seems to foster positive chemical changes in the brain, and perhaps throughout the entire body.

Gratitude and Your Health

Social scientists, psychologists, and the medical community are beginning to understand that the "emotion of gratitude" is increasingly linked with improved human health, wholeness, and well-being, and the "practice of gratitude" helps lower stress, alleviate depression, and appears to reduce a host of reported physical symptoms.

The research clearly demonstrates that the practice of gratitude makes people happier, healthier, and more productive. Gratitude reduces stress, improves the quality of sleep, and makes people (even strangers) increasingly want to assist and help you. (Highlights from the Research Project on Gratitude and Thankfulness, Robert A. Emmons, UC, Davis Investigator)

More than optimism, hope or compassion, gratitude has one of the strongest links to improved mental health and satisfaction with life. People who experience gratitude cope more effectively with everyday stress, recover more quickly from illness and enjoy more robust physical and psychological health.

Many of the effects from an attitude of gratitude are more than anecdotal—they are quantifiable. Consider this: in controlled studies, people who kept gratitude journals were 25% happier, slept one half hour more per night and exercised 33% more each week than subjects who didn't keep gratitude journals.

Groundbreaking breaking research has demonstrated that people—those who regularly practice and cultivate gratitude—experience a multitude of psychological, physical, interpersonal, and spiritual benefits, including:

- Increased ability to cope with stress
- Increased feelings of energy, alertness, enthusiasm, and vigor
- Improved cardio health
- Significant reduction in blood pressure
- More success in achieving personal goals
- Increased sense of self-confidence and self-worth
- A sense of closure in handling traumatic memories

All in all, studies confirm that those who acquire and practice 'the attitude of gratitude' experience multiple advantages; the practice of gratitude helps solve problems in our lives by helping us to heal the past, provide contentment in the present, and deliver hope for the future.

Gratitude and Your Relationships

When people report feeling grateful, thankful, and appreciative in their daily lives, they also feel more loving, forgiving, joyful, and enthusiastic. Perhaps not surprisingly, the family and friends, the partners, and others who surround these grateful people, consistently report that those who practice gratitude are viewed as more helpful, more outgoing, more optimistic, and trustworthy. (Emmons & McCullough, 2003)

Gratitude is important not only because it helps us feel good but because it also somehow inspires us to "do good." Gratitude is both internally and externally beneficial; at the same time, its positive energy impacts both others and ourselves.

Studies have shown that when people experience gratitude, they feel more loving, more forgiving, closer and more connected to people. In addition to these increased feelings of connectedness, these studies have revealed that the practice of gratitude also leads to the following:

- Robust and secure social relationships
- A greater sense of purpose and resilience
- Preponderance of generosity and helpfulness

Author, researcher, and UC Davis professor, Dr. Robert Emmons says, "Gratitude gives life its meaning." Emmons backs up his claim with eight years of intensive research on gratitude in his best-selling book, *Thanks! How The New Science of Gratitude Can Make You Happier.*

"Without gratitude, life can be lonely, depressing and impoverished," said Emmons. "Gratitude enriches human life. People are moved, opened and humbled through expressions of gratitude."

Perhaps one of the most important aspects of Emmons' research is finding that gratitude is not just a positive emotion that can improve overall health and wellbeing. "What's remarkable," he reports, "to cultivate and experience the benefits of gratitude, people are virtually compelled to give up their *victim mentality* and relinquish any sense of entitlement or deservedness."

Gratitude and Personal Performance

In other studies, one of the more surprising findings was that gratitude is positively linked to the ability to achieve and maintain personal goals, and a "grateful disposition" was a predictive indicator of future academic achievement.

Participants who kept gratitude lists or journals were more likely to make positive progress toward all their important personal goals, including academic, interpersonal and health-based objectives. (Sheldon and Lyubomirsky, 2006; Emmons & McCullough, Tsang, 2003)

Gratitude has considerable value in assessing (and predicting) "human social functioning." For many, another person's outward thankfulness acts as a subtle, yet tangible moral barometer and is often seen as a reliable and "foretelling indicator" of the possible levels of productivity, rapport, and empathy with another person—even a stranger.

It seems clear, that if nurtured, the practice of gratitude can improve emotional and physical health—it can strengthen relationships, improve academics, elevate energy levels, energize, inspire, transform—and even help prevent illness.

Gratitude and Your Business

One of the principal rules of business is, "find a need and fill it." Is it possible that communicating an attitude of gratitude in business could be profitable?

The simple truth is, almost everyone receives considerably more flak than gratitude—leaving people hungry for genuine appreciation and thanks. Customers, co-workers, vendors, family, friends, and individuals everywhere are suffering from a "severe gratitude deficit disorder." The gratitude-to-criticism ratio is out of balance.

Unfortunately, most of us are outstanding complainers. When someone doesn't meet our expectations, we are keen to let them know. On the other hand, when things go as we expect, we often don't notice or even acknowledge it. Instead, we tend to take excellence, kindness, and thoughtfulness for granted.

The gratitude gap needs filling. People want to know that they matter, that their efforts are making a positive difference. People want to be acknowledged. Is it possible that acquiring an internal and external culture of gratitude could make your business more profitable?

When employees and coworkers notice that you thank them for their efforts, they'll naturally tend to work even harder to please you in the future. They may even start thanking YOU for your excellent work!

The simple truth is: Gratitude is good business!

Gratitude and the Law of Attraction

Several years ago, I was enjoying a weekend business conference in Dallas with several hundred fellow entrepreneurs. During an afternoon break, I joined a small group of friends seated on couches in a central area of the convention hotel. Nearby were the hotel lobby bar, shops, restaurants, and a few hundred people milling about waiting for the next session.

After some general conversation, one of my close friends and I began enthusiastically telling our group about a "gratitude exercise" we had recently experienced at a workshop in Orlando. Someone asked if we'd demonstrate, so my friend and I began guiding the group through the simple instructions:

(1) All participants take their turn and speak for a moment to every other person in the group, one at a time.

(2) When taking your turn, you are to look directly at the other person and tell them what you appreciate about that person. Even if someone in the circle is a complete stranger to you, find something, at least one thing about him or her that you appreciate.

(3) Begin by telling that person *directly*, "What I appreciate about you is _____," (and not *indirectly* such as, "What I admire about Bill is _____.")

All in all, it took our little group about ten minutes to complete the exercise. Afterward, the one or two who were at first holding back, reported later that he or she was, "impacted beyond their expectations." In their way, each of the group described a positive change of state and an experience of connectedness, happiness, love, deep relaxation, peacefulness, and an unexpected joy.

What was especially remarkable—although our group was relatively quiet, and not trying to draw attention in any way—was that in the short time it took for us to complete the exercise, we inadvertently attracted thirty to forty curious strangers. The comments and questions from the "newly drawn" included, "What are you doing? Who are you? What's going on?" And, "We noticed this incredible energy coming from you people. Can we play too?"

By itself, this admittedly unscientific example doesn't prove that "practicing gratitude" in a group setting invokes the law of attraction. However, after experiencing this exercise numerous times, I've witnessed that whenever there is this kind of group expression of strong, positive emotions, it has an explicit energy that is palpable, recognizable, and very attractive to others. And for those who have little or no interest in connecting with others, the exercise doesn't seem to attract them at all.

Dr. Joe Vitale, one of the gifted teachers and authors featured in the movie, *The Secret*, says,

> "Gratitude is one of the most powerful feelings you can have. Gratitude sends a powerful signal to attract people to you, and to attract more for you to be grateful for."

> "Feeling real gratitude, being grateful for something—is one of the "missing secrets" to the law of attraction,"

he adds. "Be grateful and pretend you already have it. Add the feeling as if what you desire is already here. Feel *that* emotion, and you are engaging the law of attraction to bring you even more."

Vitale calls the feeling of gratitude, "a critical attractor factor" to which we should all pay much more attention. Likewise, William Town, in 1920 claimed, "Thought is powerful only when backed by strong feeling. Feeling gives thought its reactiveness. To merely make an affirmation of what you desire without faith or feeling, will accomplish little."

In 1966, Dr. Joseph Murphy wrote about "Our infinite power to be rich," and exclaimed, "The whole process of mental, spiritual, and material wealth can be summed up in one word: Gratitude."

The Gratitude Challenge: "Remembering to Remember."

A French proverb states that gratitude is, "the memory of the heart." And we must, "Remember to Remember." Gratitude is a choice, not always easy, but at the same time one of life's most vital ingredients. Cultivating the habit of sharing gratitude in our lives allows us to flourish — yet it can be a difficult habit to accomplish. Gratitude is easier said than done. It rarely comes without some real effort. And because gratitude is both a virtue and skill, it requires some measure of mental discipline.

One of the best ways to cultivate and develop the habit of gratitude is to establish a daily practice to remind yourself of the gifts, the grace, and the benefits of all the good things you enjoy. Importantly, each time you make "the choice for gratitude" the next time will be a little easier, a little freer, and even more automatic.

Sarah Ban Breathnak wrote: "You simply will not, you cannot be the same person two months from now after consciously learning to give thanks each day for the abundance that exists in your life." Choosing gratitude opens each of us up to the limitless possibilities for all the fullness that life has to offer.

It's easy to be grateful when life is going according to plan. But when there is a challenge or crisis in our lives, most of us retreat into the old habits of the self-absorbed, self-centered, and unappreciative in our thoughts and actions. Our minds seem to have this built-in tendency to notice and pay attention to what is going wrong, rather than what is going right. Somehow we either ignore or take for granted the many blessings of life, but instead, we quickly jump at the chance to harp or complain about what irritates us.

Neuroscientist, Rick Hansen, suggests, "Our minds are Velcro for negative information, but Teflon for positive information. We know we shouldn't complain, but we do it anyway. We know what we should do …so why don't we just do it?"

Psychologists call this "knowing, yet not doing" or the "knowledge to performance gap." We profess gratitude, yet at other times we somehow find ourselves filled with the spirit of entitlement. We *forget* to write a thank-you note. We *forget* common courtesies. We *forget* to acknowledge and thank the people who have generously helped or supported us.

Gratitude does matter. Gratitude is important. But how can we get more of it? How can we create the habit of gratitude? What can we do to rediscover and to sharpen and maintain our appreciation tools? How can each of us acquire and maintain the *Habitude of Sharing Gratitude*?

Eight Gratitude Exercises That Work!

The following exercises are useful and efficient. Several of these exercises, particularly 'gratitude journaling' and the 'gratitude letter' have been tested and proven through multiple scientific studies. All have demonstrated very positive benefits, perhaps even spectacular benefits [my words] for the participants.

It's extraordinary, at least to me, when you examine the relatively small time commitment compared to the significant return on your time invested.

Try one, or try them all and see for yourself.

(1) Gratitude Journaling

Time Commitment: Five to ten minutes every day, ongoing

The evidence from multiple studies has demonstrated that gratitude journaling (at least once a week or more) results in significant emotional and health benefits for those who are willing to develop the habit and commit to it.

Oprah Winfrey has repeatedly exhorted her television audiences with the amazing benefits you can expect from the simple daily act of "counting blessings by way of gratitude journaling."

Some of the more significant research is summarized in Robert Emmons' book, *Thanks! How the New Science of Gratitude Can Make You Happier* (Houghton Mifflin, 2007). Emmons and his colleagues at the University of California at Davis are among the pioneers in research investigations on the benefits of gratitude.

Emmons' book reports on multiple gratitude studies. For example, participants in the "gratitude group" felt much better about their lives overall, were more optimistic about the future, and reported fewer health problems than the participants in the control group. Results from a second study suggested that *daily* gratitude writing led to a greater increase in gratitude than *weekly* practice.

Another surprising study reproduced these results with a group of people suffering from various neuromuscular diseases, including post-polio syndrome, and individuals with symptoms of chronic fatigue syndrome.

Again, those using *daily* gratitude journals reported more satisfaction with their lives and were more optimistic about the future than the control group. Interestingly, they also reported getting more sleep, spending less time awake before falling asleep, and feeling more refreshed in the morning.

Researchers at the University of Connecticut also found that gratitude journaling can have a protective effect against heart attacks. After studying people who had experienced one heart attack, the researchers found that those patients who recognized the benefits and gains from their heart attack, such as becoming more appreciative of life, experienced a lower risk of having another heart attack.

Summarizing the findings from studies to date, Emmons says that those who practice gratitude journaling and grateful thinking "reap many positive emotional, physical and interpersonal benefits." People who regularly keep a gratitude journal report fewer illness symptoms, feel better about their lives as a whole, and are more optimistic about the future.

One interesting outcome is that many participants continued to keep gratitude journals months and often years later. It appears that the benefits of gratitude journaling tend to make it self-sustaining—and the ongoing external incentive is no longer required.

How to begin your gratitude journaling:

There is no need to buy an expensive personal journal or to download an app to record your entries. The important thing is to establish the *daily habit* of paying attention to "gratitude-inspiring events" and then *recording the event in writing*. Writing down your blessings translates your thoughts into words and has proven advantages over "thinking the thoughts." Writing seems to help you organize your thoughts, accept your personal experiences, see the possibility of blessings instead of burdens, and place them in a context.

1. Set aside the time each day to record a few things for which you are grateful. (Typically, people list three to five.) For the first few days find and write down one or two blessings.

2. Find a time that is consistently available—such as at the end of your day, before bedtime or right after you awaken. Choose a time that helps reinforce your new habit.

3. You can write in a book such as the "Journal of Gratitude" (available at bookstores or on Amazon books) or write on loose-leaf paper or a notebook. In my opinion, it's easier to write on paper than to write electronically, but what's most important is that you enjoy and maintain your new habit, whatever method you choose.

4. Begin to establish the daily practice of "paying attention to gratitude-inspiring events" then write them down when you journal. Intention leads to the discipline of writing—and discipline produces results. Learn to expect nothing but appreciate everything!

5. Specificity is necessary. When you say you are grateful for someone, why is that specifically? Rather than saying, "I am grateful for my wife", say, for example, "I am grateful for my wife because she has told me she loves me every day for the past twenty years." With gratitude and gratitude

journaling, the benefits seem to increase when you add more detail and feeling.

In Emmons' words, the act of writing, "helps you see the broader meaning of events going on around you and helps create meaning in your life."

Finally, save your gratitude journals! My dear friend, Marilyn Lahr, has been keeping a gratitude journal for over twenty years. She says, "My journals from the past are among my most sacred treasures. They offer me the opportunity to look back and see my journey—the person I was, the person I've become, the healing I've experienced."

A traditional Hausa (West African) saying offers this: "Give thanks for a little, and you will find a lot."

(2) The Quick-Start: Five Minutes A Day:

Time Commitment: Five minutes a day for seven days

If you're not ready to commit to journaling yet, you can still increase your long-term happiness by almost 10% with this simple, five-minute exercise.

Here's the exercise: "At the end of your day, write down three things that you are grateful for and why you are grateful. (Three things that went well, for example.)

We spend tens of thousands of dollars on expensive electronics, homes, automobiles, and vacations hoping for a small boost in our feeling of happiness. This exercise offers a free alternative, and it works!

Again, try it for a week and see for yourself!

In a study of this exercise's effectiveness by Martin Seligman, participants were asked to follow these instructions for seven days. After only one week the participants were 2% happier than before. But, in follow-up tests, the group's happiness kept on increasing from 5% after one month, and to 10% after six months.

It's interesting to note that although participants were instructed to do the "three gratitude exercise" daily for a week, many of them enjoyed the benefits so much they continued doing it on their own indefinitely.

(3) Visualization: Seeing Your Gratitude

Time Commitment: Ten to twenty minutes per week

The good thing about visualization is that you can practice it almost anywhere and anytime you have a few moments to spare. You can close your eyes when you're waiting in the doctor's office for an appointment, or keep them open anytime you are waiting in line.

As with any exercise, you can practice it longer or more frequently if you want to experience a faster and more powerful change in your life.

Visualize and picture in your mind someone for whom you are grateful. Say out loud (or in your mind) a few specific reasons why you are thankful for that person. List all the reasons you are thankful that they are in your life. The more details you add to the visualization, the better.

You can focus your gratitude on one person, and use it as a way to profoundly increase the appreciation you have for your spouse or any other important person in your life. Remember, ingratitude can destroy marriages and relationships. Perhaps practicing gratitude can strengthen and save a marriage.

(4) Powerful Gratitude Prayers (non-denominational)

Time Commitment: Two to four minutes each day

Prayer is an especially powerful technique for cultivating gratitude because prayers can provide you with the exact words to say, specific things to be grateful for, and a person (or entity) to be grateful for.

It's interesting to note that every religion has some form of ritualized prayers of gratitude, and without fail, all faiths, across all cultures, consider gratitude an important virtue. Virtues, by the way, are synonymous with their practitioner's happiness. Another way to say this is, the virtue of gratitude, among other virtues, helps create happiness.

Here are a few short, non-denominational prayers. Try these, or create your own. If ever you needed any reason to pray, now you have one. Gratitude helps make you and others happy, not to mention the other benefits we've already related.

A Simple Prayer of Thanks: I am grateful for my family and friends, a job to earn my keep, and the health to do it, and opportunities and the lessons I've learned. Let me never lose sight of the simple blessings that form the fabric and foundation of my life; I am blessed, yesterday, today and tomorrow. (© Abby Willowroot)

Earth's Abundance Prayer: Before me is proof of Earth's abundance. Before me is evidence that I am most fortunate. Before me is a meal, many millions can only dream of, with hunger in their bellies that I am blessed not to feel. May I savor each bite that nourishes me. May I never take this plentiful bounty for granted. May I use this fuel given to my body, wisely and well, and never squander my blessed life on petty things. Before me is the proof of Earth's abundance;

may I never fail to remember how truly blessed I am. (© Abby Willowroot)

There are many books available on Amazon that feature gratitude prayers. One of my favorites is *Gratitude Prayers: Prayers, Poems, and Prose for Everyday Thankfulness,* by June Cotner.

(5) The Gratitude Visit

Time Commitment: 1-2 Hours

One study revealed that writing and delivering a gratitude letter produced the greatest sustainable increase in overall happiness compared to almost any other gratitude-improving methods.

Plan a 'gratitude visit' with a friend, a former teacher, a co-worker, family member, or someone you appreciate greatly. Think of a person who has made a difference in your life or perhaps someone to whom you have never fully expressed your thanks.

In advance of your visit, write a one-page letter to the person listing all the reasons you appreciate them. Be specific about how and why they have made a difference in your life, and why you are so thankful to know them.

Take your time writing your gratitude letter. Be creative and think of specific details about that person or your relationship, why you are grateful, and how you have benefited tangibly, emotionally or materially, and how they have positively influenced your life.

If possible, meet him or her in person and avoid telling the person about the purpose of your visit in advance. Take the letter with you and read it out loud. Afterward, give them your letter as a keepsake.

If for some reason you can't meet in person, then a gratitude visit by phone can be the perfect substitute. Consider sending your gratitude letter to the individual as a unique remembrance (rather than emailing, which is less personal).

(6) The Gratitude Date

If you're open to experiencing a wonderful date with your significant other or spouse, follow the gratitude visit instructions, write a letter to him or her and take it with you to dinner, a picnic, on vacation, or any other time the two of you can be alone together.

Read the letter out loud—then hand them the letter to keep. I guarantee it will turn out to be one of the most memorable and well-received gifts you've ever offered your loved one, spouse or friend.

As I was writing this chapter, I initiated gratitude visits with a former client and friend, a childhood friend, and a gratitude date with my amazing wife, Penny. The experience, the feelings of joy and contentment, the positive energy and connectedness, are worth a hundred times the few minutes it takes to write the letter and plan the date.

Take the opportunity and enjoy the extraordinary benefits of a gratitude date. Afterward, if you feel like sharing your story, I'd honestly love to hear about your experience.

Feel free to email me at montetaylor@mac.com

(7) The Virtual Visit: It's Never Too Late

Abraham Maslow said, "It is vital that people count their blessings to appreciate what they possess, without having to undergo its actual loss." Unfortunately, sometimes we don't take advantage of the opportunity to tell people how much we appreciate them—or how grateful we are—until they are gone from our lives.

I've often wished I would have had a gratitude visit with my father before he passed. It eventually occurred to me that I could write my letter and have a virtual gratitude visit instead. I decided to write a letter to my father as if he was still living. I found one of my favorite pictures of him and a comfortable spot to be alone with my letter, his picture, and my memories, and began reading.

I'm not sure Monte Sr. heard me, but it felt to me in some way that he understood and appreciated my visit. Moreover, the act of writing and reading it aloud rekindled in me the remembrance of his beautiful spirit, and aroused the deep thankfulness I have for all the love, the times (and laughs) we shared when he was still alive.

Thornton Wilder said, "The highest tribute to the dead is not grief—it is gratitude. Faith Baldwin reminds us, "Most of us forget to take the time for wonder, praise, and gratitude until it is almost too late. Gratitude is a many-colored quality, reaching in all directions. It goes out for small things and for large; it is God-ward going."

If someone you love, someone you miss, has passed, find the time to write that person a gratitude letter. Enjoy a virtual visit and read your letter out loud. It's a simple expression of your enduring love, and it will fill your soul with pleasure. And remember too, your soul is always touching others.

The Power of Sharing Gratitude: In Conclusion

Gratitude as a skill, and as an attitude, is foundational. It is often called "the first language of the heart." Once you are infused with the habitude of feeling and expressing gratitude, it becomes surprisingly easier to speak the other languages of the heart: love, courtesy, kindness, forgiveness, encouragement, withholding judgment, listening, empathy, joy, and peace, to name a few.

In the next chapter, you'll discover how gratitude is also one of the most powerful indirect facilitators for achieving and expressing the next habitude—and one that could easily be called the "second language of the heart."

CHAPTER TWO

The Habitude of Embracing Forgiveness

The weak can never forgive. Forgiveness is an attribute of the strong. –Mahatma Gandhi

The First One Was The Right One

Some people have a formidable gift for helping others see what they haven't been able to see before; Leyland Val Van De Wall was one of those extraordinary life-teachers. "Val" is what his students and friends called him.

Whenever Val held a workshop, he purposely set the stage by placing a sizeable whiteboard and at least two tables at the very front of the room, and within his reach. On them, he carefully positioned hundreds of personal items: dog-eared newspaper and magazine articles; photos; keepsakes; cartoons; books; trivia and notes—so at any moment he could grab one of his 'props' to emphasize a point, share a laugh or introduce a supporting idea.

He was a full-on spiritual tutor, a professor with a knack for entertainment, patrolling his stage like a wily method actor, carefully leveraging his memorabilia while serving up his personal brand of "show and tell." A master of timing—he thoughtfully guided the tempo of learning to allow everyone adequate time to digest the more challenging concepts and philosophies he put forward.

I vividly recall one weekend when Val read a short newspaper article that reported the alarming statistics for divorces in North America. "Show of hands," he asked. "How many here are married?" More than half of the room raised their hands. "Don't be shy," he challenged. "Stand up if this is your second marriage, third, or more."

Tittering and laughing, a surprising number of individuals arose while the others looked around to count the members of the 'multiple marriages club.' I too raised my hand and stood.

Pausing momentarily for effect, Val announced firmly, "Everyone standing, please listen carefully. It's critical that you understand this." Then he wrote and underlined the following words on his whiteboard: <u>The first one was the right one</u>!

Val turned back around and asked if everyone in the group could see what he had written. Although I wasn't aware of it at that very moment, I later realized he was waiting to see who would be the first to take some offense or question this astonishing declaration. I could sense the confusion-charged atmosphere in the whispers and murmur from the audience. Since no one seemed to have the courage to confront him, Val tossed out his "oral bait" once again:

"In case you're not clear, let me repeat. If you have remarried, you should know that the first one was the right one. Your first marriage was perfect for you!"

Visibly distressed and her voice wavering, one woman began to protest. "Mr. Van De Wall, I'm upset. I don't know why you would say this to us. My second husband Dave is sitting here next to me. We've been happily married for sixteen years, and he's a lovely man. My first husband was a total jerk."

And what followed were several minutes of the woman's emotional (and somewhat entertaining) confession of her previous husband's sins.

Val listened patiently, inviting her to continue.

"How could you possibly tell me my first husband was the right one?" she asked again.

"Because ... he *was* the right one," Val answered, as if his argument was utterly unassailable.

"Your first husband and all the people in your life are there for a reason—and one of the most important reasons is so that as a spiritual being, you can learn everything you need to know about compassion and love and forgiveness."

(It's important to be clear—Val didn't want to hurt anyone's feelings. His entertainer-teacher side purposely invited the minor drama, and as he confessed later, "I wiggled a few brain cells to capture your attention and create a learning moment.")

Forgiveness: The Second Language of the Heart

Val asked us to carefully consider that every single relationship in our life is the *right one* for that moment of time. "You must entertain the possibility that *life is a school* that contains all the things you need to know about being fully human."

"After twelve or more years of education, you may have learned how to diagram a sentence or argue the square root of pi. However, you have typically studied nothing about the real power of forgiveness, or what can happen to your lives and your health if you hold on to anger, hatred or recriminations. The school of *all about your life* is always in session — and your schooling ends when your life ends," he added.

By challenging us with, "the first one was the right one" Val implored us to learn that every relationship in our life has a gift for us — no matter how frustrating, disappointing or painful it seemed at the time.

For our spiritual advancement as human beings, we must learn to look back, learn to let go of the hurt or anger, and to the find the parts of that relationship for which we can be grateful. The power of learning to be *grateful for the lessons* leads to forgiving-ness: forgiving our self, and forgiving others.

Again: "Let us not look backward in anger, nor forward in fear, but around us in awareness."

Val would continue to invite discussion and then probe. "What was the gift, the lesson that helped you grow and evolve so you could become the kind of person who is capable of attracting the love of your second husband? What was the connection that led you to the next, and then to the next, and forever changed your life for the better?"

Un-forgivingness is an unyielding human chain that impacts not only our self but also all other relationships in our life — and its destructive effects inexorably flow downstream through generations of families and lives. Angry, hurt, resentful, unhappy, depressed — then your school is still in session. The first one was the right one because of *that* experience, *that* relationship or circumstance. Regardless of any pain or suffering, your experiences are an indispensable link in the evolutionary chain of your life's journey.

"Your first husband (or wife) was one of your great teachers—you should send him or her flowers to say thank you," Val suggested.

Acknowledge all your "hurtful relationships" as a gift and release the hurt with a sense of gratitude. Gratitude is the surest path to forgiveness, and forgiveness leads to understanding and ultimately to joy and peace. Val helped us see, perhaps for the first time for many of us that day, that gratitude and forgiveness are two sides of the same coin of the human spirit, and as a coin—inseparable. Gratitude helps us to forgive; forgiveness engenders gratitude; each leads to the other.

You'll know you've arrived when your anger or hurt begins to diminish, perhaps even disappear forever.

It's true that many of Val's students learned how to forgive that day, and as unlikely as it may seem, several decided to acknowledge the many lessons learned from a previous relationship by sending *the first one, who was the right one*, a gift of flowers!

The Science of Forgiveness

Decade's worth of research on forgiveness has arrived at a common conclusion: forgiveness is not only healthy for our minds and bodies—it's healthy for our relationships too. And happily, the benefits of forgiveness may go well beyond the positive consequences generally suggested in the domains of psychology and health.

University studies involving hundreds of graduates across two continents reported that acts of forgiveness improved the student's performance measured via physical fitness tasks. In contrast, participants who recalled incidents marked by a lack of forgiveness and *failing to forgive* demonstrated noticeably reduced performance measured by evaluative fitness tasks.

Researchers speculate that a state of un-forgivingness is like carrying a heavy burden—a burden that victims bring with them when they navigate the physical word. Forgiveness can *lighten* this heavy load. It was noted that victims who are unable to reconcile with their offenders feel a sense of powerlessness. Withholding forgiveness may decrease the availability of physical resources (blood glucose, for instance) that could otherwise be used to cope with physical challenges such as jumping or climbing a hill. Perhaps forgiveness leads to increased feelings of personal power, which manifest themselves in greater physical strength.

Another study evaluated the effects of self-forgiveness and self-compassion. The researchers carried out an experiment involving healthy young adults who were asked to endure "standard unspecified laboratory stressors" and have their stress levels measured before and after. Participants with higher self-compassion and self-forgiveness demonstrated significantly lower levels of stress as measured by testing the concentration of an inflammatory agent linked to stress, interleukin-6 (IL-6). Test subjects with lower self-compassion and self-forgiveness exhibited significantly higher baseline stress levels, especially when subjected to anything annoying.

The study findings suggest that 'self-compassion and self-forgiveness,' and 'letting yourself off the hook' may serve as a protective factor against stress-induced inflammation and inflammation-related disease. It's important to note that psychological stressors and the resulting inflammation were linked to multiple diseases including cancer, heart disease, Alzheimer's and other neuronal disorders.

The Stanford Forgiveness Projects are the largest research-tested methods for forgiveness ever conducted.

(www.learningtoforgive.com). The powerful therapeutic model combines guided imagery, stress management and 'personal story-therapy' to help people unravel the grievance process. The program teaches that pain and disappointment need not control you.

The project's research findings reveal that forgiveness isn't wishful thinking—it's a trainable skill—and a method for forgiving almost any conceivable hurt. It demonstrates that forgiveness can significantly improve a person's physical and emotional wellbeing, and restore a victim's sense of personal power.

Some researchers propose that forgiveness dramatically changes an individual's biological equilibrium. Advanced scientific tools offer us the ability to go beyond self-reporting questionnaires, interviews and group sessions, and help scientists more accurately measure neurobiological responsiveness. New studies assess blood pressure, heart rate, emotional imagery, facial EMG, and skin conductance to evaluate enhanced therapeutic outcomes related to forgiveness and its opposite: un-forgivingness.

There is an outpouring of new data and information focused on measuring the effects of forgiveness on stress, happiness, coping with major illness, alcohol and drug abuse, grief, loss, violence, marital distress, divorce, relationships, intergroup conflict, and post-traumatic stress disorders.

These are only a handful of the hundreds of completed studies on the science of forgiveness. The majority of these projects are considering how forgiveness can enhance physical, mental and spiritual recovery. The results confirm the social and psychological benefits of forgiveness and relationship restoration.

Most importantly, they are seeking to determine the very best methods to foster forgiveness development as a positive and beneficial behavioral strategy.

The Choice To Forgive: An Inner Decision

Many of the greatest philosophers and teachers, countless books, scriptures from the bible and other religious texts single out forgiveness as one of the most important values of life. Forgiveness is an essential teaching in Taoism, Confucianism, Christianity, Judaism, Islam, Buddhism, and a critical component of virtually all spiritual practices.

For those who have experienced terrible tragedies at the hands of others—intentional or unintentional—forgiveness seems contrary to all logic. How can one possibly forgive physical or mental abuse that has occurred for years? How can one let go of a betrayal that has disintegrated a family, or violence and hatred that have destroyed lives? And what about those times when we are the betrayer, the perpetrator of an action or event that has harmed others or ourselves?

Anger, hurt feelings, guilt, resentments, hatred and self-loathing are strong feelings—emotions that are likely to visit each of us sooner or later—and a natural part of the great human experience called living. But anger, resentments, hatred, and un-forgivingness has dire consequences, as Frederick Buechner described so powerfully:

> Of the Seven Deadly Sins, anger is possibly the most fun. To lick your wounds, to smack your lips over grievances long past, to roll over your tongue the prospect of bitter confrontations still to come, to savor to the last toothsome morsel both the pain you are given and the pain you are giving back—in many ways it is a feast fit for a king. The chief drawback is that what you are wolfing down is yourself. The skeleton at the feast is you.

And this description from an illuminating Buddha text:

> Holding on to anger and resentment is like grasping a hot coal with the intent to throw it at someone else, but you are the one getting burned.

Few people realize the tremendous positive impact *one's ability to forgive* has on their happiness and health. How can we learn to access enough love, self-love, and empathy for others in order to experience the benefits of better physical, spiritual and mental health and greater happiness? How can we learn to offer, accept and ultimately embrace forgiveness, perhaps even pass it on to our children as an enduring legacy?

Part of the answer rests in accepting our humanness. Humans are the great choosers! Regardless of how we may feel at times—we are not born to lose—we are born to choose and to live with our choices. It is a fundamental truth that man, unlike any other creature on earth, has the unique and extraordinary power of his mind, freedom to choose and to decide how he ultimately feels about anything.

Nowhere is the power of this freedom described more clearly than in Dr. Victor Frankl's stirring account of his experiences in Nazi prison camps during World War Two. He wrote: "All of the familiar goals in life were snatched away from the prisoners" until what alone remained was the very last of their human freedoms: *the ability to choose one's attitude in any given set of circumstances.*

In the final analysis, it became apparent to Frankl, regardless of the physical and mental horrors, that the sort of person each prisoner became was the result of an *inner personal decision*, and not the result of camp influences alone. Under any circumstances, every man has the extraordinary individual power to decide what shall become of him mentally and spiritually.

The ability to access our "ultimate power" begins the moment we realize that *no one makes us happy or sad*—and our emotions don't happen to us as much as *we choose them*. The Greek truth-seeker, Epictetus declared that all unhappiness arises from our futile attempts to control events and people—over which we have no power—and this ongoing and useless endeavor weakens the body and leads to disease.

The pathway to our ultimate power is through our choices!

One of the great inner duals of life is between choosing to let go and forgive, or choosing to maintain our hatreds, resentments, anger, hurt feelings—and refuse to forgive. Dismissing forgiveness stultifies our happiness, our peace of mind, our productivity, our body and our very health; it is insidious as it drags us down into loneliness, poverty, despair—and even death.

Mother Teresa offered humbly:

> People ask me what advice I have for a married couple struggling in their relationship. I always answer: pray and forgive. And to young people from violent homes, I say: pray and forgive. And again, even to the single mother with no family support: pray and forgive.

And from the Lords' Prayer (Christianity):

> Forgive us our trespasses, as we forgive those who trespass against us.

Also:

> Forgiveness is not the misguided act of condoning irresponsible, hurtful behavior. Nor is it a superficial turning of the other cheek that leaves us feeling dazed and martyred. Rather, it is the finishing of old business that

allows us to experience the present, free of contamination from the past. – Joan Borysenko, Ph.D., from *Fire in the Soul: A New Psychology of Spiritual Optimism.*

And what Martin Luther King, Jr., once wrote about Jesus' command to love your enemies:

Forgiveness does not mean ignoring what has been done or putting a false label on an evil act. It means, rather, that the evil act no longer remains a barrier to the relationship. We must recognize that the evil deed of the enemy-neighbor, the thing that hurts, never quite expresses all that he is. An element of goodness may be found even in our worst enemy.

Now we can see what Jesus meant when he said, "love your enemies." We should be happy that he did not say, "like your enemies." It is almost impossible to like some people. "Like" is a sentimental and affectionate word. How can we be affectionate toward a person whose avowed aim is to crush our very being and to place innumerable stumbling blocks in our path?

How can we like someone who is threatening our children or bombing our homes? That is impossible. But Jesus recognized that love is greater than like. When Jesus bids us to love our enemies, he is speaking of understanding and creative and redemptive goodwill for all man. Only by following this way and by responding with this type of love are we able to be children of our Father who is in heaven.

So, if you're open, ready—willing—and able, let's look at several forgiveness exercises that can offer guidance: some to help forgive yourself, and some to help you forgive others.

Forgiveness Exercises That Work!

For this simple exercise to work best, it's important to understand that there are *two layers of forgiveness*. The first layer relates to the person we resented, judged, or perhaps even hated. (The person we need or want to forgive). And the second layer is even more subtle; it is about *forgiving ourselves* for having judged, hated or resented the person we need or want to forgive in the first place.

To fully access and 'clear' both layers, commit to *forgiving the person* – and importantly, commit to *forgiving yourself*. This simple technique is very effective. You can say it out loud or say to yourself. Either way, the key is to have the courage and willpower to say it.

Say to yourself, "I forgive (fill in the blank for the name of the person place or thing you judged, hated or resented) and say, "I forgive *myself* for judging, hating or resenting (fill in the blank for the name of the person place or thing you judged.)"

Say it once or say it as often as you need. You decide. You'll know it's working when you start to notice the level of emotion and negative sensations you previously felt begin to subside.

You'll begin to feel great peace.

The secret to handling all the injustices, all your grievances, all your blunders, all your failures, all your resentments, all hatred, bitterness, and disappointments—is to release them—because the truth is the only existence they can have is in *your mind*.

"You know you have forgiven someone when he or she has harmless passage through your mind." –Reverend Karyl Huntley

The Nine Steps To Forgiveness

The Nine Steps To Forgiveness have been taught successfully to tens of thousands of people worldwide via workshops, conferences, church groups, and seminars. The revolutionary program has helped countless people learn how to put blame in the past, change the way they feel in the present and learn to handle anything that comes their way.

Fred Luskin, the director of the Stanford Forgiveness Projects, advises, "Forgiving someone does not mean forgetting or approving of hurtful events in the past. Rather, it means letting go of your hurt and anger, and not making someone endlessly responsible for your emotional wellbeing. It does not mean condoning someone's actions, or even forgetting what had happened."

One of the most important aspects of the program is helping people recognize the self-defeating trap of "unenforceable rules." Like making a new rule that gravity will no longer affect you, these unenforceable rules are 'self-created things' that we are powerless to turn into a reality: such as the desire to change something that has already happened in the past, or the desire to control other people's behavior.

"There are no miracle cures for life's struggles," offers Luskin, "But we have found in our research that forgiveness can reduce stress, blood pressure, anger, depression, and hurt; while forgiveness can increase people's optimism, hope, compassion, and physical vitality. Like many things, forgiveness requires practice to perfect, but with this practice, it becomes stronger and easier to find. It takes a willingness to practice forgiveness day after day to see its profound benefits for physical and emotional well-being."

Step One: Know exactly how you feel about what happened and be able to articulate that what happened is not OK. Then, share your experience with a few trusted people.

Step Two: Make a commitment to help yourself to feel better, and know that your forgiveness is for you and no one else.

Step Three: Recognize that forgiveness does not necessarily mean *reconciling with the person who upset you nor does it mean condoning the action*. Through forgiveness, you are seeking the peace and understanding that comes from dropping the blame and taking offenses less personally.

Step Four: Get the right perspective on what is happening by recognizing that your distress results from the hurt feelings, thoughts, and the physical upsets you are feeling *now*—not from what offended you or hurt you two minutes, or ten years ago.

Step Five: Whenever you feel upset, practice stress management techniques to help soothe your body's 'fight or flight' response.

Step Six: Give up expecting things from your life, or from other people that they do not choose to give you. Remind yourself that you can desire better health, love, friendship, and prosperity, and work hard to get them. However, these are *unenforceable rules*: you will suffer when you demand that these things occur since you do not have the power to make them happen.

Step Seven: Rather than using any experience that has hurt you to achieve goals, use your energies to find other ways to meet your positive goals.

Step Eight: Remember that a 'life well lived' is perhaps the best revenge. Instead of focusing on your wounded feelings and giving power to the person who caused you pain, learn to look for the love, beauty, and kindness around you. Put your energy into appreciating what you *do* have rather than mourning about what you *don't* have.

Step Nine: Reframe and revise the way you view your past and remind yourself that the 'heroic choice' is to forgive.

Helpful hint: I found it very useful to consider the rules individually—one at a time—by writing and numbering each of the nine steps on the front of a large index card. On the back of each card, I wrote personal notes, my thoughts, and commitments related to the rule on the front. By taking a few minutes each day, you can sort through, reflect, and then reaffirm your commitments.

Remember this:

> When we harbor negative emotions toward others or ourselves, or when we intentionally create pain for others, we poison our own physical and spiritual systems. By far the strongest poison to the human spirit is the inability to forgive oneself or another person. It disables a person's emotional resources. The challenge is: to refine our capacity to love others as well as ourselves and to develop the power of forgiveness."
>
> Caroline Myss, PH.D. Excerpted from *Anatomy of the Spirit: The Seven Stages of Power and Healing*.

Forgiveness Letters and Heroes

Writing a forgiveness letter is a powerful tool and one that gives you the opportunity to express your feelings about the person, the event, and any pain you feel or any emotions you are still experiencing. The choice to send the letter—or not—is yours and yours alone. Remember, forgiving doesn't mean that you deny the other person's responsibility—nor does it minimize or justify the wrong. You can forgive the person without excusing (or pardoning) the act.

Joseph Campbell, the great author and intrepid student of Jungian psychology suggested: "Everything is forgivable, but not necessarily pardonable. The only unpardonable sin is the sin of inadvertence, of not being alert, not quite awake." Campbell, in his unique way, was admonishing us to be fully conscious of life's possibilities and to wake up and feel the rapture of being fully alive.

Learning to forgive, or paying the steep price for not doing so, is one of the great human themes that weave through mankind's history and consciousness. Campbell and Jung both argued that forgiveness is one of the prerequisites to enlightenment—perhaps the first step of any hero's journey.

Forgiving is a difficult business. When someone you cared about, or still care about, hurts you, you can hold on to anger, resentment, bitterness and even revenge—or you can make a choice to embrace forgiveness and move your life forward towards a path of physical, emotional and spiritual well-being. True forgiveness offers you the possibility of bringing a beautiful and gentle peace into your body that helps you move on with your life.

As George R. Melton believed: "Of one thing I am certain, the body is not the measure of healing—peace is the measure."

One of the most important objectives of your letter is to write an *explicit statement of forgiveness*. This physical act allows your mind and body to feel what it's like to express *and experience* complete and utter forgiveness. Actively choose to forgive the person who has hurt you, even if they are no longer living or in your life. Many people never send the letter, but writing it can help clarify everything in your mind.

Writing a forgiveness letter is a 'heroic opportunity' to move away from your role as a victim—and ultimately release any power or control the event or the person had over your life. It takes time and no small amount of courage, but the results are worth it.

"*For Giving*" declares that you are all for the act of giving—you are in favor of giving. Forgiving another also means being in favor of giving something back to yourself. Understand and know that by writing your forgiveness letter you are honoring yourself.

The forgiveness letter is FOR YOU!

Forgiveness Hawaiian Style

I first learned of the "Ho'oponopono forgiveness exercise" from an audio series I listened to several years ago. (*The Ultimate Law of Attraction Library,* by Dr. Joe Vitale.) I'm a devoted fan of Vitale's work, and I'd highly recommend listening to this series, especially if you're a teacher, coach, mentor, psychologist, therapist, committed to helping others, or improving yourself.

(On a side note, I fully credit Joe Vitale for indirectly encouraging me to write and complete my first book, *Objections Handled! Learn To Say The Right Things To Every Prospect*. I was jogging early one morning in Scottsdale, Arizona, listening to one of his recordings, and something Vitale said, one of the stories he shared, helped clarify and catalyze my resolve. I decided that within the year I would once and for all write and publish a book that could make a positive difference in the lives of the readers. Less than a year later I sent Dr. Vitale a copy of my book and added a short thank-you note. I was surprised and honored a week later when he sent me a very encouraging email, "You've accomplished what few have, congratulations, keep going!")

The meaning of 'Ho'oponopono' is defined in the Hawaiian Dictionary as, "mental cleansing: and family conferences in which relationships are set right through prayer, discussion, confession, repentance, mutual restitution, and forgiveness." The powerful intention of Ho'oponopono is to put things to rights; to put in order or shape, to correct, revise, adjust, amend, regulate, arrange, rectify, tidy up, and make orderly or neat. In a way, you could say that Ho'oponopono is all about making things right…. And then letting go.

Vitale reported that when he first heard the story of how Hawaiian psychologist, Dr. Ihaleakala Hew Len, was reportedly healing mentally ill patients by using a Ho'oponopono exercise, he imagined it was some form of scam. Vitale couldn't let the thought go—so eventually he investigated and spoke with Dr. Len and the hospital staff.

He learned that Dr. Len never met physically with his patients, but instead quietly read the patient charts and focused deeply and mentally on each of them, forgiving them and forgiving himself by repeating, "I'm sorry. I love you," over and over again until his patient's health improved. Vitale reported to his great surprise that Dr. Len's methods had helped patients who once had no chance of ever being released, and many were eventually freed. (For more information about Ho'oponopono, please go to http://www.healingstars.com/healing-tools/forgiveness-ho-pono-pono/)

In addition to forgiveness, I've found that this 'Ho'oponopono exercise can be a very useful mental clearing technique for anytime you experience any of those occasional "life or people frustrations." Dr. Vitale's adaptation goes like this: "I'm sorry, please forgive me, thank you, I love you." It is one of my favorite clearing exercises.

I've been jogging almost daily for over 35 years, and as most outdoor exercisers know, sooner or later you're going to cross paths with a leash-free animal or a distracted or texting driver (who runs you off the road). There are even some folks who think it's entertaining to fling things at runners and bikers from a moving car.

After one of these interactions, I need a little mental Ho'oponopono clearing to stay positive. I'm not complaining, but recalling a few of these experiences suddenly brought up a strong need to say, "I'm sorry, please forgive me, thank you, I love you!"

Whew. Now I feel better!

If this story of "Ho'oponopono forgiveness" surprises you, or if you're skeptical, I understand. Perhaps this small piece of wisdom from Carl Jung will help: "Being human, there will be some things we must accept on faith, while now and then we must even indulge in speculations."

Carl Jung, Joe Vitale and I would like you to have some faith—please try Ho'oponopono—I believe you will be happily surprised!

Twelve Forgiveness Principles To Get You Unstuck

Jack Kornfield, the acclaimed author, renowned psychologist and teacher of Buddhist psychology, explains how one can tap into the great human capacity for forgiveness—even when you're feeling stuck! In the Buddhist tradition, Kornfield teaches that forgiveness—although it can be—is *not particularly* about the other person. Forgiveness is about the beauty of your *unique soul* and your personal capacity to fulfill your life.

As humans, we have the extraordinary capacity for dignity and forgiveness—providing we can find a way to get in touch with it. "Forgiveness doesn't mean that you necessarily have to speak or even relate to the person who betrayed you," Kornfield cautions. "It's not about them. It doesn't condone their behavior—your forgiveness can stand up for justice and say 'no more'." As the Bhagavad Gita says, "If you want to see the brave, look to those who can return love for hatred. If you want to see the heroic, look to those who can forgive." It's not easy. "Love and forgiveness are not for the faint-hearted," wrote Meher Baba, the Indian mystic.

But someone has to stand up and say, "It stops with me; I will not pass this sorrow on to my children." Someone has to say, "I will accept the betrayal and the suffering, and I will bear it, but I will not retaliate. I will not pass this onto the next generation—and to endless generations of grandchildren."

Kornfield's 12 Forgiveness Principles:

> (1) Understand what forgiveness is and what it is not: It's not condoning; it's not a papering over; it's not for the other person; it is not sentimental.

> (2) Sense the suffering in yourself, of still holding onto this lack of forgiveness for yourself or another. Start to feel that it's not compassionate; that you have this deep suffering that's not in your best interest. So you actually sense the weight of not forgiving.

> (3) Reflect on the benefits of a loving heart. Buddhist texts say, "Your dreams will become sweeter; you will awaken quickly. Men and women will love you, angels and devils will love you. If you lose things, they will be returned. People will welcome you everywhere when you are forgiving and loving. Your thoughts become pleasant. Animals will sense this and love you." Elephants may even bow as you go by—try it at the zoo!

56

(4) Discover that it is not necessary to be loyal to your suffering. This realization is big. We are so loyal to our suffering, focusing on the trauma and the betrayal of "what happened to me." OK, it happened. It was horrible. But is that what defines you? "Live in joy," says the Buddha. Look at the Dalai Lama, who bears the weight of the oppression in Tibet and the loss of his culture, and yet he's also a very happy and joyful person. He says, "They have taken so much. They have destroyed temples, burned our texts, disrobed our monks and nuns, limited our culture and destroyed it in so many ways. Why should I also let them take my joy and peace of mind?"

(5) Understand that forgiveness is a process. There's a story of a man who wrote to the IRS, "I haven't been able to sleep knowing that I cheated on my taxes. Since I failed to fully disclose my earnings last year on my return, I've enclosed a bank check for $2,000. If I still can't sleep, I'll send the rest." It is a self-training, a process, layer by layer—that is how the body and the psyche work.

(6) Set your intention. There are complex and profound teachings in Buddhist psychology about the power of both short-term and long-term intention. When you set your intention, it sets the compass of your heart and your psyche. By having that intention, you make obstacles surmountable because you know where you are going, whether it is in business, a relationship, a love affair, creative activity, or in the work of the heart. Setting your intention is critical and powerful.

(7) Learn the inner and outer forms of forgiveness. There are meditation practices for the inner forms, but for the outer forms, there are also certain kinds of confessions and making amends.

(8) Start the easiest way, with whatever opens your heart. Maybe it's your dog, and maybe it's the Dalai Lama, or maybe it's your child—whichever thing or person that you most love and can forgive. Then you bring in someone who

is more difficult to forgive. Only when the heart is all the way open do you take on something difficult.

(9) Be willing to grieve. And grief, as Elizabeth Kubler-Ross describes it, consists of bargaining, loss, fear, and anger. You have to be willing to go through this process in some honorable way, as I'm sure Nelson Mandela did. Indeed, he described how, before he could forgive his captors, he was outraged and angry and hurt and all the things that anyone would feel. So be willing to grieve, and then to let go.

(10) Forgiveness includes all the dimensions of our life. Forgiveness is work of the body. It's the work of the emotions. It's the work of the mind. And it is interpersonal work done through our relationships.

(11) Forgiveness involves a shift of identity. There is in us an undying capacity for love and freedom that is untouched by what happens to us. To come back to this true nature is the work of forgiveness.

(12) Forgiveness involves perspective. We are in this drama called 'life' that is so much bigger than our own little stories. When we can open up to this view, we see it is not just our suffering it is the suffering of humanity. Everyone who loves will be hurt in some way; everyone who enters the human marketplace gets betrayed. The loss is not just your pain—it is the pain of being alive.

Note: You can access a remarkable video of Kornfield guiding you through the *12 Principles of Forgiveness* by searching that title on YouTube.

Another Perspective On Forgiveness

I am so grateful for having the opportunity to attend workshops and classes some years ago with an extraordinary teacher, Kath Kvols—the founder of International Network for Children and Families (INCAF). Kath is the author of several books, including the outstanding, *Redirecting Children's Behavior*. Through the years she has hosted workshops and training for thousands of teachers, nurses, counselors, childcare workers, and parents.

Through Kath's life-skills and parenting workshops, I gained a unique perspective on forgiveness that has only broadened in its usefulness over time. Kath had a gentle, deeply loving (and relentless) ability to challenge and persuade many hurt, angry, bitter and resentful people, to *momentarily* set aside their blame. She encouraged people to pause, to consider, and take responsibility *for one thing* in the relationship. It could be anything large or small the person (may have) contributed to 'co-creating' the circumstances or event that needed forgiving in the first place.

Her technique was to invite the person to "try on the possibility" even if it didn't fit. Here was the extraordinary lesson: at almost the very moment a person was willing to recognize and accept that they had a part—and honestly acknowledge their part, large or small—the difficult path to forgiveness and reconciliation was less obstructed and more attainable.

Did this strategy always work? No, but it often did—and it offered a valuable insight into the complex dynamics of life relationships. How much more wisdom and healing are possible once we are *completely open* to the knowledge that each of us contributes at least *some part* of our failed relationships? This idea is not to direct blame towards anyone, but instead to redirect us to take at least *some* personal responsibility for the outcome. By doing so, we have the opportunity to replace our 'victim-ness' with power, and to exchange our bitterness for compassion, understanding, and peace.

By taking responsibility, we have the opportunity to reclaim our personal power.

A Short Personal Story

There are times from my life where I can see (now) that I was completely mistaken about "who caused whatever to happen" and I almost left out the following story because, in hindsight, it seems so ridiculous. There was a twisted complexity: it took me some time to realize that there was no need to forgive the other person because I created everything. I was so busy blaming others I couldn't see the facts clearly. Once I saw the truth of the experience—the only person I needed to forgive was myself!

What follows is an ordinary story about a teenager beginning to figure things out. No lives or arms or legs were lost. No one's psyche was irreparably harmed—although at the time, and for several years later—remembering the details was painful and embarrassing.

While in Catholic school, around age eight, I started music lessons for both piano, and later the guitar. And in my early teens, I started playing the trumpet so that I could march with the band. In my last year of junior high school, another trumpet player challenged me for the first chair position, one I'd held for almost two years. I lost the challenge and had to slide down to the second chair and give up my comfortable and long-held throne.

Disappointed, I lobbed an inappropriate zinger at the band director, Mr. Snyder, who responded by ordering me out of his band room. Later that day I discovered what he meant was I was "out" for the remainder of the school year. Humiliated and embarrassed, I explained to the vice-principal and anyone else who bothered to ask, "It was entirely Mr. Snyder's fault. He made me accept the chair-challenge before I was ready." My excuse was I had broken my right arm several weeks before while skiing, and I was still uncomfortable playing my horn, even though the cast had been removed. The real truth was I hadn't bothered to practice my trumpet in many months.

My counselor, Mr. McKinney, helped me move my classes around so I could instead join the school choir in the mid-year. Moreover, over a period of several weeks of discussion, he helped me realize that whether Mr. Snyder had overreacted or not, I had created the event. I was the person *solely* responsible.

Looking back many years later, I'm very grateful that Mr. Snyder had the gumption to take a stand. He wasn't angry or mean. He calmly instructed me to get out of his class—for the rest of the year. And over time, one of the important lessons I learned was to be more careful about the words that seemingly flow out from my mouth—especially when I'm feeling angry or hurt.

The point is, at times the most important person any of us needs to forgive is one's self. It's so easy to play the victim by blaming someone else. We are all human. We all make mistakes. But the only way to learn and grow and mature—and reclaim our power—is to abandon our "victim-ness." Always blaming others means always being the victim.

Acknowledge your part and forgive yourself. Be grateful for the lesson.

The moment we can see *our* contribution large or small, and the part *we* played in creating any of life's dramas or controversies, we begin to experience the joy and satisfaction that radiates from authentic personal power.

The Power of Embracing Forgiveness: In Conclusion

There is a staggering amount of research material dedicated to the scientific study of forgiveness. Scientists are now beginning to recognize its therapeutic benefits: we know forgiveness can help people create healthier relationships, improve the immune system and overall health, reduce anxiety, stress, and hostility, and lead to greater spiritual, physical, and psychological well-being.

It's important to note that a fundamental analysis of the research suggests that while some people can forgive at the drop of a hat, forgiveness, for most, is a process that takes some time. Everett Worthington, an acclaimed researcher at Virginia Commonwealth University, stated: "A factor as simple as the *amount of time someone spent trying to forgive*, is highly related to the actual degree of forgiveness experienced."

It seems that authentic forgiveness often requires patience and perseverance. The following paragraph from the Christian Science Monitor offers this inspiration:

> When it comes to forgiveness, Jesus is the greatest exemplar. If anyone had the right to be angry, it was he, because, after a lifetime of blessing others, he was crucified. While on the cross, however, he said, "Father, forgive them, for they know not what they do" (Luke 23:34). He petitioned for the forgiveness of those who crucified him, and he harbored no resentment. It's hard to imagine he could be so forgiving after having been treated so grievously, but understanding his motive is an important key to being able to forgive anything and everything.

Science, it now appears, is helping to verify the great wisdom and knowledge of the ages: forgiveness is one of the most beautiful and powerful heart languages.

Perhaps more any other balm or medication—forgiveness can heal us!

Val Van De Wall hugging our dear friend Cindy Tabor—San Diego, circa 1990. Little did we know at the time that both would pass away in a few short years.

Bethany Alkazin, Val Van De Wall, and my wife Penny Taylor—
Hawaii, circa 1990

CHAPTER THREE

The Habitude of Fearless Listening

"Listening is music to another's heart. It is the unspoken melody of empathy, understanding, and connection; a heart language that requires no words."
—*Monte Taylor*

Oprah's 'Aha' Moment

In 2011, Oprah Winfrey released a commemorative magazine issue titled, *Behind the Scenes of 25 Incredible Years*. This extraordinary edition featured the inside details for twenty-five of Oprah's "greatest lessons learned" from over two decades of hosting her Emmy award-winning television show.

She reported that one of her most significant interview moments took place during a 1993 show that highlighted the relationship therapist, Harville Hendrix, Ph.D.

Audience response to his interview was so enthusiastic, and Oprah was so enthralled, that she invited Hendrix to come back later and conduct five full weeks of 'live couple's therapy' on the show. Ultimately, Hendrix made eighteen appearances throughout the show's broadcast lifetime.

For the most part, the Hendrix, *"Getting the Love You Want"* sessions focused on helping married couples understand and heal painful relationships. Each session began with Hendrix guiding the guest couples through their critical first lesson, which was an exercise on how to demonstrate and convey deep empathy, *simply by listening to the other person very carefully*.

As Oprah watched, Hendrix taught the couples a method of listening that was very distinct from what most of us practice. Instead, he coached sincere and humble listening; this is listening without judgment, without reservation, without negativity, without criticism, and listening without defending or blaming.

He proposed and taught a form of listening so rare and foreign, so difficult for most people—one might even call it "fearless listening."

Specifically, it is listening intently—with open-minded curiosity—without any other agenda or purpose. "Curiosity," Hendrix claimed, "is the secret to great couple communication." He noted how infrequently we are *curious enough* to listen to one another carefully.

"Although couples typically report that they *hear* each other," he says, "most people have fundamentally lost the ability to *listen humbly* and *quietly* to one another."

Oprah later reported that the most striking outcome of the exercises appeared at the very moment either partner finally got it right. By listening—and with no other purpose than to fully understand their partner's perspective, pain, or point of view—there was a sudden shift, a palpable sense of empathy and harmony. This small change created an immediate feeling of positive, healing energy.

"What I learned completely impacted my relationship with my partner, Stedman," she reported. Later, Oprah attributed the very survival of their relationship to the best-selling author's revealing insights on listening.

So, why would an exceptionally talented and attentive host like Oprah have a "listening epiphany"? Anyone who has watched Oprah would agree that she's an excellent listener. So, what was it she learned from Hendrix that was so different from the kind of listening she practiced daily on her show?

The answer lies in the word *agenda*. Oprah discovered that it's nearly impossible to achieve deep, personal empathy with another person when you come to the table with a predetermined motive that may be contrary to the other person's needs.

There are so many details required to develop and deliver a daily hour-long broadcast. It requires a meticulous plan guided by production constraints—scheduling commercials; prearranged questions; topics and talking points. And while the interviews may seem relaxed and natural, always running below the surface is a strict production schedule that forces Oprah's team to communicate with an *underlying agenda*, and the goal is to create entertainment value for her viewers.

However, watching the couple's sessions, Oprah witnessed the interpersonal miracles—the transformation that is possible—providing one is willing to surrender to the discipline of listening with no predetermined outcome. She recognized the incredible healing power of deep listening— listening only to understand what another person is feeling. She experienced what is possible when one person is willing to offer their unbiased ear to someone else—without interruption, comment, manipulation or even fear.

Fearless listening is the very genesis of creating, strengthening, or reconciling human relationships. The willingness to listen deeply and fearlessly to one another—without reservation—creates an environment for empathy. And empathy is perhaps the most powerful bonding experience couples can have.

From a human perspective, empathy is one of the surest paths to trust. Empathy restores connectedness and union. Empathy enriches relationships. The hallmarks of "lazy listening" are distractedness, apathy, indifference, self-absorption, and self-serving motive—all which serve only to weaken or destroy relationships, create confusion, conflict, and separateness.

The hallmarks of fearless listening are unbiased engagement with another, listening without expectation and without striving for an outcome, and creating the soul-enlivening doorway to empathy and trust.

Regardless of how highly any of us might currently rate our listening skills, it's clear that everyone can benefit from learning how to become a more skilled listener—perhaps even a heroic listener.

The Red-Headed Step-Child of Communication Skills

The practice of listening is the neglected stepchild of personal skills—and humans pay little more than lip-service to its care and feeding. Typically regarded without the favor of birthright, most people will agree that while listening is important, it's a brand of personal hygiene that *others* should practice more often.

If you'd like to experience a group of people in near universal agreement, take the stage in front of an audience. Then say, "Folks, if you agree with the following statement made by Steven Covey, please raise your hands up high."

"Most people do not listen with the intent to understand; they listen with the intent to reply."

Without fail, almost everyone's hands will rise. Some people will laugh and lift both hands. If you want to have some more fun, ask the folks who didn't raise their hands, if any, to verify that they disagreed—by standing up. Repeat the statement, and more often than not, after some laughter and confusion, you'll soon discover they weren't listening carefully to either the directions or to the Covey quote, and that's the reason they didn't raise their hand the first time.

Covey, the late author of the brilliant research study and resulting book, *7 Habits of Highly Effective People*, noted, "Communication is the most important skill in life. We spend years learning how to read and write, and years learning how to speak. But what about listening?"

Skillful listening is arguably one of the most important abilities for effective communication—it is the most basic and perhaps the most powerful way to connect with another human being. Most of us would say, "Of course; I know that already." But knowing is not the same as owning the information and following through with action.

As Tony Robins reminds us, *"Information without execution leads to poverty."*

So Why Don't We Listen?

Beyond our excuses and rationalizations, there are logical, obvious and even surprising science-based reasons why it's hard for most of us to be good listeners.

Careful listening is hard work

Offering someone our complete attention is an act of will; it requires that we work against the inertia of our own self-absorbed, distracted minds. Frankly, most of us aren't willing to do the hard work. Because it's often easier be casual about listening, if not complacent, many people are fundamentally lazy listeners.

Careful listening is an acquired habit

Poor listening and deep listening have at least one thing in common—they are both acquired habits. Unfortunately, we humans seem to love our habits more than any reason to change, even if changing would be good for us. The late Val Van de Wall warned his students, "You don't have your habits—your habits have you." And Samuel Johnson observed, "The chains of habit are too weak to be felt until they are too strong to be broken."

We're busy-busy

The issue of busy-ness has spawned the adjective, "time-starved." Thus, we have the time-starved parent, executive, employee, child, butcher, baker, and candlestick maker. Contrary to what most people believe, a closer analysis reveals that we have even more free time today than at any other time in recorded history—up to several more hours per day! Perhaps it's not that we have less free time than in the past, but what we have instead is option overload.

We're distracted

We multitask with our mobile devices, social media, Twitter, Facebook, YouTube, television and binge-watching House of Cards on Netflix. (Guilty!) We plug into our music, our mobile device, our internal dialog, our self-talk, personal, family, and financial needs, and then, of course, there are all those important and not-so-important emails.

We're disinterested

Sometimes we're not attracted to the topic or captivated by the individual. Assaulted by so much information, hype, and commercial messaging, we often require something unique and out-of-the-ordinary to slap us back to attention.

Sharing is much more of an opiate than listening

Telling others how we feel, and how we think, triggers the same sensations of pleasure in the brain as food, money, and sex. By monitoring brain synapses in human subjects, Harvard scientists discovered, that, "self-disclosure feels so rewarding at a cellular synapse level, most people can't stop themselves from sharing their thoughts."

Findings published in the Proceedings of the National Academy of Sciences noted, "Subjects were often willing to forgo money rewards in favor of talking about themselves." Perhaps now we can better understand the copious over-sharing on Facebook and Twitter.

Human brains are naturally thrifty

"Thin-slicing" is a term made popular in the book, *Blink*, by Malcolm Gladwell. It refers to our human tendency to make quick decisions with tiny amounts of information. Deep listening is difficult for us because it runs counter to the way our brains have evolved to function. The brain's *natural tendency* is to evaluate input quickly, predict outcomes, and make judgments, and to perform "informational triage" on a moment-to-moment basis. Our inherent need to jump to a conclusion and decide *right now* has at least some scientific justification.

Our brain prefers what it expects

Language researchers and psychologists have discovered that our brain continually compares any incoming information against what it already knows. Our brain organizes and prioritizes this "incoming noise" and seeks an expected context for the stimulus. The meaning it typically uncovers relies heavily on our personal bias. In other words, the brain discovers what it expects to discover.

Scientists point out that what people *already think they know* usually outweighs what the incoming information or signal appears to be saying. Hence the snarky comment, "I've already made up my mind—please don't confuse me with the facts!" To a surprising extent, the structure of our expectations, both conscious and non-conscious, largely determines much of what we see, hear and feel. The great Denis Waitley was fond of saying to his audience, *"Guess what? You get what you expect."* And now brain scientists seem to agree.

We have little or no formal training in listening

Even though most of us spend more than half of our day listening, research shows that listening—as a communication activity—receives the least amount of instruction in our education. Listening training is neither offered nor required in most of our schools. One study revealed that students taking a *required* communications course spent less than seven percent of class time learning about listening. Business and academic professional continually cite listening as one of the most critical skills for professional effectiveness—yet *less than two percent* of either business or academic journals deal with its effectiveness.

A survey of thousands of graduates from over a dozen full-time MBA programs—conducted by a leading business school accrediting body—found that graduates rated one-on-one communication as the single most important workplace skill. However, only six percent of the graduates rated their business school even moderately effective in helping them develop in this critical area.

Our diminishing attention span

According to the National Center for Biotechnology, in a little more than a decade, the average attention span for an adult in the United States is down almost thirty percent. The average "arc" of our attention is diminished—from about twelve seconds in 2000—downward to an average of about eight seconds in 2013! (Interestingly, eight seconds is roughly one second less than the measured attention span of a goldfish.)

We typically stop and check our email boxes about every two minutes throughout the day, and about twenty percent of the time we spend less than five seconds on any single Internet page view.

Media research claims that the average person hears more than 30,000 television commercials a year—and the majority of those messages are between fifteen to thirty seconds long. Could it be that our attention span is gradually and imperceptibly being entrained to listen in shorter bursts and ever-shrinking sound bites?

We don't realize the actual benefits of profound and careful listening

Multiple studies demonstrate that listening-related abilities such as understanding, comprehension, open-mindedness, supportiveness, and empathy constitute the *single most influential dimension* upon which people make judgments about the communication competencies among friends, family, co-workers, teams, and leaders. It seems that the *language of listening* perhaps indicates love and caring more clearly than any other communication, or as Barbara Nixon observed, *"Listening is the hug you give with your mind."*

Empathetic listening requires a willful override of our brains' favored modes of operation—and of our deeply ingrained habits. In a world of constant multitasking, digital distractions, multi-entertainment options, and information overload, listening is a complex skill we are in danger of losing.

Taken together, we now know that interference, apathy, the pull of brain opiates, our natural human tendencies, plain old laziness, and not fully understanding the advantages of listening and paying attention are a handful of the many reasons why we don't listen as well as we possibly should.

The Business Case for Better Listening

In business, listening is one of the most critical abilities for by which employers and co-workers judge workplace competence. A Wall Street Journal survey of more than 2000 corporate recruiters reported that "Interpersonal communications skills are what corporate recruiters crave most—but find most elusive in MBA programs."

Human resource professionals continually rank listening as one of the top "soft skills" necessary for entry-level positions. They also rate listening as *one of the overall top skills* driving employee advancement and promotion.

Listening and oral communication skills universally rank higher in HR professional decision-making (hiring and promotion) than any other skills; such as problem-solving, enthusiasm, self-motivation, written communication, technical competence, and GPA/academic performance.

Contrary to popular cultural belief, most top sales trainers teach—and top performing salespeople have learned that effective personal selling is about listening and asking questions, not talking *at* or *to* the customer. It's interesting to note that many top salespeople are introverts who know how to put their egos aside, stop talking, and keep their ears open.

Corporate leaders continually rank the ability to listen as one of the uppermost leadership and performance characteristics of top CEOs, executives, managers, and administrators.

In business, it's important to note there are also gender-based listening issues. Multiple studies show men continually marginalize women in meetings and conversations. Sociologists Don Zimmerman and Candace West discovered that men listening to women, tend to interrupt 33% more often than when they are listening to another man.

Low morale: Studies show that one of the primary reasons employees choose to leave a company includes the poor interpersonal skills of a supervisor or co-worker, with reported poor listening ability as a chief complaint.

How Listening Impacts Academic Success

A student's academic success in school is more often associated with effective listening than with any other personality dimension.

Multiple studies show that over 66% of the students ranking high on listening tests became honor students after the first year as opposed to 4% of those scoring low on listening tests.

Most universities do not offer listening training as part of the curriculum. In one study, 49% of students scoring low on listening tests were on academic probation within the year, while only slightly more than 4% of students scoring high on listening tests were on academic probation.

Doctor: Are You Listening?

On average, physicians interrupt sixty-nine percent of all patient interviews *within eighteen seconds of the patient beginning to speak*. In seventy-seven percent of the doctor-patient interviews evaluated, the doctor failed to elicit the patient's actual reason for visiting.

The *most significant* indicators of patient satisfaction are the doctor's or the attending healthcare worker's behaviors related to empathy and listening.

Research shows that the most important skill in the doctor-nurse, nurse-patient, and the doctor-patient relationship is communication. Two-thirds of all health-related malpractice suits are ultimately linked to a breakdown in communications.

Health-care professionals, who listen attentively, express empathy, ask open-ended questions and involve the patients in decision-making, significantly increase the overall patient satisfaction as well as the patient's *willingness* to carry out the prescribed treatment.

Listening: The Path To Better Parenting (and Happier Children)

Most child psychologists agree that when children feel right, they'll behave right; and to help children feel right we need to understand and acknowledge their feelings. Accepting another's feelings is called empathy, and the surest path to understanding is listening intensely.

While children certainly thrive on words of encouragement and praise, listening deeply to children helps boost their self-esteem, enables them to feel worthy and loved, and helps them build a healthy self-concept. Listening may very well be the highest form of encouragement for our children.

Children understand language long before they can master speaking it. One of the best ways to keep up with a child's evolving language skills and its development is by paying daily, regular, focused attention on the child—by listening.

Regardless of a child's age, when we ignore our children by not listening, we send the message that "What you have to say isn't that important." What children feel is, "Mom (or Dad), *I'm not important to you*." Active communication with young people means paying attention, respecting the child's feelings, watching your tone of voice, and taking a moment to listen deeply and without an agenda.

Years ago, Robert Fulghum, author of *Everything I Need to Know I Learned In Kindergarten,* remarked, "Don't worry that your children may never listen to you; worry that they are always watching you."

And, what are they watching you not do? *Not listen.*

Listen! Important advice for parents, or anyone who strives to nurture children!

Robots or Doctors?

In the 1970's, IBM researchers ran a revealing experiment. The study was designed to learn which was the most rewarding experience for humans. Was it patients talking to doctors—with the typical 'doctor allowed' time to speak? Or was it patients talking to robots—with 'unlimited robot time' for the patient to speak their mind?

The patients overwhelmingly reported that the robots, seemingly with all the time in the world, and by listening patiently, offered a much more rewarding experience than the doctors.

Surprising? Maybe not!

Most of us have experienced talking with someone and thinking later, *that was one of the most enjoyable conversations I've ever had*. Then, thinking about the conversation you realize, with some embarrassment, that the other person hardly said a word. This example reminds me of the Jarod Kintz quip, "We talked for four hours. Well, I talked for four hours, and she listened for two."

The conversation felt great to me. How did it feel to you?

One of the greatest gifts we can offer—especially to someone we care about—is our complete attention and a listening ear. William James suggested this, "The deepest principle in human nature is the craving to be appreciated."

What simpler way to show our appreciation for someone than by listening carefully and humbly?

Listening without interruption is one of the most tangible and authentic ways to show another person how much you value them. Karl Menninger expressed it so beautifully when he said, "Listening is a magnetic and strange thing, a creative force. The friends who listen to us are the ones we move toward. When we are listened to, it creates us, makes us unfold and expand."

The commitment to openly listen to another person is an act of will—an act of heroism. The Greek etymology of the word 'clear' means 'like a window'. It means something that allows all of the light to enter directly—without obscuring or interfering with the light.

Exercises: From Lazy Listening To Fearless Listening

Here are four very powerful exercises that will help you make dramatic improvements in your ability to connect with others, and help you master the art and science of listening. One of the most important themes to remember as you begin is this: "Most people don't want a good talking-to—what they want is a good listening-to."

The Delayed Response

The "delayed response" exercise is a great place to start—and one of the easiest ways to noticeably begin to improve your skills.

Try this: Whenever someone finishes speaking, or seems to finish speaking—pause and wait—don't say anything at all for several seconds. (I usually make a slow, silent count to five or six.) This unique and surprising pause will send a powerful message to the other person that you are gathering your thoughts and have been listening intently to their communication.

My good friend, and best-selling author, Alex Theis, often uses this strategy in conversation. Of one thing you can always be sure: Alex is listening.

The delayed response exercise is surprisingly useful for both personal and business conversations and will help the person speaking feel that you are thoughtfully considering their ideas, concerns, and most of all, are truly tuned-in.

Because silence is so uncommon—the rarity of it can be very alluring. Pausing, or saying nothing, while being present in the moment, sends a clear message that you are accepting the person who is talking. Staying quiet doesn't mean that you approve or agree with everything that he or she is saying; it only means that you are glad they are sharing.

Stay In Your Lane

Imagine a two-lane road with the painted line separating the lanes down the middle. In the left lane see the words: defending, blaming, explaining, and rationalizing. In the right lane see the single word: learning. Make sure to stay in the right lane—and avoid passing, and crashing headlong into anything and everything that turns up on the left.

As the speaker warms up and gets comfortable talking, even if it's an uncomfortable subject, listen attentively and silently. If you begin to feel you can't contain yourself if you don't respond a little, nod and say, "Hmm," or, "I see."

Margaret Wheatley argues, "Listening is such a simple act. It requires us to be present—and that takes practice—but we don't have to do anything else. We don't have to advise, or coach, or sound wise. We just have to be willing to sit there and listen."

Find the strength to refrain from offering your wisdom! Continue to provide brief statements or phrases that let the person know you're pleased he or she is talking and sharing, but most of all, let them know, "I am eager to hear more."

Here are a few examples of phrases or statements you can use:

"Please continue. I'm very interested."

"It means a lot to me that you're sharing your viewpoint."

"You're doing an excellent job describing what happened."

"Could I trouble you to repeat that? I want to be sure I understand what you're saying."

"It sounds like you have a lot on your mind."

"Hmmm. Please tell me more."

And if you have trouble remembering to stay in your listening lane, just know this: "A good listener is not only popular everywhere, but after a while he knows something." – Wilson Mizner.

Interested—Not Interesting

If you're willing to do an Internet search, type in the exact text of one of the more famous Dale Carnegie quotes, and you will be presented with over 170 million results on Google. The quote is, "*'You can make more friends in two months by being interested in other people than in two years of trying to get people interested in you*," from the famous *How to Win Friends and Influence People*—one of the first best-selling, and most successful self-help books ever published.

Written by Dale Carnegie and first published in 1936, the book has sold over 15 million copies worldwide. What's surprising is how many people still don't practice one of its fundamental secrets—one of the absolute best tried-and-true methods for conveying and demonstrating your interest in another person.

It's straightforward: Ask people questions and *listen* carefully and quietly to their response. Let the response lead you to more thoughtful questions. Be interested in what the person is communicating. And don't worry, if you do little more than ask a few questions to demonstrate your interest—and then listen without interruption—most people will find you *very* interesting.

Author Brian Tracy, arguably one of the greatest personal and business development teachers, adds this small twist, "'You can make more sales in two months by being interested in people's businesses, than in two years of trying to get people interested in your business."

Want some experience some magic? Then try this: Make a *regular practice*, once a week or more, of slipping into your "interested rather than interesting" mode. You can practice at home with your children, your spouse, at parties, business mixers, and in almost any social situation. You can practice it on phone calls.

Here are a few examples of phrases or questions will help you get started:

"I'm wondering…"

"I'm curious…"

"Would you be willing…?"

"Tell me about…"

"Would you mind if I asked you a question about…?

"What are you working on now that you're excited about?"

In his insightful book, *Just Listen—Discover The Secret To Getting Through To Absolutely Anyone*, Psychiatrist Mark Goulston writes about the extraordinary power of using the simple phrase, "Hmmm…" to help you listen more attentively to someone. "When you deeply listen," he says, "and get where people are coming from, and then care about them when you're there, they're more likely to let you take them where you want to go."

"People have their needs, desires, and agendas," Mark adds, "…and they're stressed, busy, and often feeling like they're in over their heads. To cope with their stress and insecurity, they throw up mental barricades that make it difficult to reach them—and one of the secrets to getting through is *just to listen*."

I recently had the opportunity to hear author, Jack Canfield, deliver a live keynote presentation for an audience of eager entrepreneurs. He's the co-author of the worldwide, mega-selling, *Chicken Soup for The Soul* series. I've been a big fan of his "life success messages", of his book, *Success Principles*, and have greatly enjoyed his "how to be a top author" webinars and teleconferences.

Jack Canfield is also a very focused and attentive listener. I had the opportunity to watch Jack as he mostly listened, and as he asked questions to a small group of fans. Later, when I introduced myself and spoke with Jack privately, I found he was mostly interested in why I was at the conference, what I was doing, my projects, what I liked best about the weekend, and so on. He epitomizes the connecting principle of "being interested" rather than trying to be interesting.

My great friend, Tom Alkazin, is a very successful entrepreneur and an extraordinary leader—in part because he's perfected the art of listening carefully to people. He gets to know people, learns what they need, and determines if in some way he can be of service. Tom has mastered the art of listening carefully, and he has helped thousands of people become more successful. He's also created hundreds of meaningful and rewarding life-long relationships along the way.

In the beginning, being interested rather than interesting requires great discipline, and a willingness to set aside your ego and briefly quell your need to express your opinion. It requires the will to "shine the light" and focus it squarely on others—and *listen*! The results and the benefits over time will likely astonish you.

"Listening is a magnetic and strange thing, a creative force. The friends who listen to us are the ones we move toward. When we are listened to, it creates us, makes us unfold and expand." —Karl Menninger

"To listen is to give up all expectations and instead give our attention, completely and freshly, to what is before us, not knowing what we will hear or what that will mean. In the practice of our days, to listen is to lean in, softly, with a willingness to be changed by what we hear." —Mark Nepo

The Triple M's for Masterful Listening

The Triple M's method employs a deceptively simple mnemonic reminder to help you remember and take advantage of the most time-honored principles for masterful listening.

The three "M" letters represent critical listening areas which you must learn (and practice) to be an active listener. The "S" is to remind you to summarize for clarity of communications.

(1) M = Mouth

(2) M = Mind

(3) M = Meta-messages

S = Summarize

The first "M" cautions you, the listener, to "control your mouth." Larry King's mouth has this to say on the subject, "I remind myself every morning: nothing I say this day will teach me anything. So, if I'm going to learn, I must do so by listening."

- Keep quiet
- Don't interrupt
- Avoid the temptation to comment
- Avoid the temptation to offer advice

If you're feeling the urge to provide a comment or some advice, ask yourself, "Is what I'm about to offer truly worthwhile? Will my comment make a significant difference to the conversation? Will my information or comments help create more understanding, empathy or closeness?" If not, don't offer it.

The second "M" reminds you to "manage your mind."

Criss Jami advises, "It's not hard to understand a person; it's only hard to listen without bias."

- Avoid judgment

- Don't jump to conclusions
- Avoid problem-solving
- Don't allow your mind to get distracted
- Stay calm and confident, even if the speaker is emotional about the topic

Here's a helpful reminder from Ralph Nichols: "The most fundamental human need is the need to understand—and be understood. The best way to know and understand people is simply to listen to them."

The third "M" reminds you to "manage your meta-messages." A meta-message is the underlying and implicit meaning, the not-so-hidden sub-text of information transmitted to one another by your body language.

"So when you are listening to somebody, completely, attentively, then you are listening not only to the words but also to the feeling of what is being conveyed, to the whole, not the part of it." – Jiddu Krishnamurti.

- Face the speaker
- Keep your attention on the speaker
- Maintain comfortable eye contact
- Don't fidget or move around needlessly
- Take notes if you want—but ask for permission first

The meta-message "M" also reminds you to be wary of what *your* body language is saying or transmitting to the speaker. Mixing an idiom with a metaphor, I'll say it this way, "Don't let your body language start running off at the mouth."

Nonverbally, with your body, face, eyes, your attention and demeanor, you should convey this feeling to the very person who is speaking: "*I acknowledge and value you. I want to understand your point of view fully; I'm very interested in what you have to say.*"

Understanding The Importance Of Meta-Messages

Multiple studies agree that in all kinds of interpersonal communications, non-verbal cues and messages, including tone of voice, *carry up to 70% of the overall meaning of communication*, as opposed to the spoken words.

Let me underscore this important fact once again: Non-verbal cues carry up to 70% of the overall message.

While the studies can debate the exact percentages, it's clear that YOUR nonverbal expressions AND the speaker's non-verbal expressions are both critical to understanding the communications.

Here's a short primer to help you decipher your speaker's body messaging:

- Is the tone of voice or underlying demeanor emotional or discouraged?
  (Changes in complexion color, red in the face or neck area; voice changes such as a change in pitch or stammering.)

- Is his or her demeanor threatening, defeated, frustrated, resigned?
  (The breathing rate or perspiration increases. The head is down or gazing at something else, picking at clothes, fiddling with a pen or sitting slumped in a chair.)

- Does their message or story seem truthful?
  (Little or no eye contact, rapid eye movements, with the pupils constricted; the hand or fingers are in front of the mouth when speaking, or the body physically turned away from you.)

Be aware that body language is more powerfully persuasive and informative than it might seem at first. "The most important thing in communication is hearing what isn't being said. The art of reading between the lines is a lifelong quest of the wise." — Shannon Adler

Then summarize (The "S" in the 3M's)

Finally, the "S" in the Triple M'S method reminds you, the listener, to summarize or reframe *any time* you want to be sure that you fully understand what the speaker is trying to communicate.

For example, "Bill, I want to make sure I understand you correctly. What you're saying is [summarize]?" Or, "Sue, your main idea or concern is [summarize or reframe]?"

You can harness the incredible power of the Triple M's method to keep you on track and moving more quickly towards mastery—and to transform you from "a lazy listener" to a "fearless listener."

The Power of Fearless Listening: In Conclusion

The challenges are clear: listening carefully to others, without bias, is hard work. Listening fearlessly runs counter to the natural tendencies of our brain's hardware. It is counter to our need to make quick decisions, so we aren't hopelessly bogged down with the millions of messages bombarding us daily.

Fearless listening is almost heroic because it takes courage; it requires work. Being a hero doesn't always mean performing some big gigantic act of heroism. Often the hero is persistent at doing a few simple things—over and over. Listening, carefully, fearlessly, and humbly dissolves the barriers between people—so it deserves your commitment—and the multiple benefits are quite profound.

Understanding someone's pains, needs, wants, dreams, and desires—and responding, is perhaps one of the most powerfully effective tools you'll ever discover for connecting deeply, and for helping you get through to the hearts and minds of others.

Develop your habitude of **fearless listening**.

Get good at it, and the richness of your experiences and relationships in your life will change magnificently. Know that the more you invest in someone else's experience, the more you might positively change your own.

Fearless listening is a rare and magnificent habitude indeed!

CHAPTER FOUR

The Habitude of Spreading Encouragement

"Too often we underestimate the power of a touch, a smile, a kind word, a listening ear, an honest compliment, or the smallest act of caring—all of which have the potential to turn a life around."
– Leo Buscaglia

Never Underestimate A Math Teacher

One of my all-time favorite teachers, Vern McKinney, understood the power of encouragement. Most students knew him affectionately as "Mr. Mac." He was the energetic 8th grade math teacher and ever-busy boy's guidance counselor at Grand Junction Junior High School.

In the early part of my first year of 7th grade, aside from girls, what particularly caught my attention one day was a flyer in the cafeteria announcing the formation of an after-school singing club. Mr. Mac, who I'd heard about, but had yet to meet, was the sponsoring teacher.

I could sing and play some acoustic guitar, so I decided to attend to see what it was all about. I didn't know at the time that my decision would lead to a more than twenty-year friendship with Mr. McKinney.

Along with forty or so other music-loving hopefuls, I was greatly relieved when Mr. Mac explained there would be no try-outs or eliminations—anyone and everyone could participate. Our group met twice a week and soon this crazy-funny-exuberant math teacher began preparing us for a winter concert as he guided us through the songs and harmonies of Peter Paul and Mary, the Kingston Trio, and the Beach Boys.

We were enthusiastic, loud, and often out of tune—and we loved every minute of it. I arrived early for rehearsals, wrote out lyrics, helped others learn the guitar chords and anything else I could do to become an important part of the group.

One afternoon, Mr. Mac asked me to stop by his office for a chat. He began by telling me how much he appreciated my energy and dedication. He said he felt I was musically gifted, and said, "You make me laugh." I thought our visit was off to a good start.

But what came next surprised me. I don't recall the exact words, but the essence of Mac's message was, "I've also noticed that when you're trying to be clever, or funny, or whatever it is you're doing, you sometimes hurt people with your words." He went on to tell me that one of my friends came to office sobbing earlier because of some comment I'd made to her. I truly didn't even remember what I'd said.

He went on to tell me that one of my teachers reported, "Monte disrupts my class with his running commentary." She calls you "motor mouth."

And if you're beginning to notice a pattern here in my early teens, you would be right. (Many years later a former schoolmate asked, "Do you remember in junior high school when everyone started calling you motor mouth"? "Hmmm," I responded with a straight face, "No, I don't recall that exactly.")

Neither Vern's words nor his methods were original, but the spirit of his intention was to encourage me—and at the same time have me recognize the consequences of what I was creating. Here was a teacher I had grown to respect and admire, looking me straight in the eye, and saying, "Monte, you have something great inside of you to offer the world— and I see it." The second part of his message was, "But you've got to learn to think about the impact your words have on people, and before you open that big mouth."

"More music, less mouth," he suggested.

It would be a delightfully ironic ending to my little story if I'd gone on to become a world-famous comedian or acclaimed musician. Neither of those things happened. And I wish I could say that from that day forward, I never again hurt someone's feelings while trying to be witty—but it's happily very rare. I'm still not always the man I want to be, but I'm also not the boy I used to be.

What's important is that I heard what he said. I accepted his recommendation and began to think more carefully about how my words made another feel. I didn't miss that important lesson because Mr. Mac somehow found a way to get through. He spoke a language I could understand: empathy, encouragement, and guidance.

It wasn't Mr. Mac's words—it was the "music of his words." It was his heart language. I started to believe in his vision for me. He recognized the signs of a better possible

Monte; a person I could barely see for myself at the time. He was profoundly instrumental in awakening my potential.

I'm hoping you had a person in your life that offered you an intriguing glimpse of what you could achieve or become. It may have been a teacher, a friend or a parent who in some way ignited your spirit—or planted in you the seeds of change.

Like Plants Need Water

Most of us can share a story about a time in our life when someone encouraged us, but encouragement is somewhat easier to describe than it is to define.

The prominent Adlerian psychologist, Rudolf Dreikurs, declared encouragement, "the single most important attribute in getting along with people." As the clinician widely credited for bringing attention to its importance, he considered encouragement to be "a chief feature of human development, and of any psychotherapeutic treatment."

Dreikurs often asserted, "Children need encouragement like plants need water." He was careful to distinguish encouragement from "praise", which he felt was not a particularly useful method for instilling courage, confidence or perseverance. Dreikurs characterized praise as a form of feedback or congratulations (for something done in the past) as opposed to encouragement, which he felt had a much greater and continuing impact on others.

He taught that encouragement was *paramount* because it engendered strengths in another that helped address the recipient's perceived limitations. He viewed encouragement as, "the process of facilitating the development of a person's inner resources and active movement or change."

For the sake of clarity, I'd like to offer this narrower definition of encouragement: "to inspire or help others find the belief that they can find solutions, can cope with any predicament and can realize almost any potential."

The Swiss Army Knife of Positive Influence

The vast majority of research literature and empirical studies confirm that encouragement is a universal tool for social support and positive influence. It is one of the most influential attributes of effective parenting, family counseling, couple and family therapy, business leadership, teaching, education, coaching in sports and all forms of effectiveness coaching.

These are some of the extraordinary and revealing benefits of positive encouragement noted in many research, scientific and associative studies:

Encouragement is positively associated with:

- Children's healthy physical outcomes
- Improved outcomes at all levels of academic success
- A teacher's ability to nurture student's academic skills
- Adherence to healthy diets and healthy lifestyle
- Improved job performance and job self-efficacy
- More efficient managerial and supervisory skills
- Elevated verbal and social persuasion skills
- Higher level of performance on mental and physical tests
- Rapid healing following medical and surgical procedures
- Healthier/more satisfying marital and family relationships
- Improved interpersonal communication
- Improved mental health/heightened sense of well-being
- A greater satisfaction of life

Beyond question, encouragement is one of the most powerful tools we can employ for positive social influence.

Additionally, it appears that the practice of encouragement yields benefits not only to the recipient but also to the encourager. These "encouraging types" of people have outcomes associated with *their* positive mental health, academic achievement, and enhanced physical health.

The "heart language habitude" of spreading encouragement could well be the ideal expression of the doctrine of "give and receive."

Magical Teachers and Mentors

If you are skeptical about your ability to positively influence or change another person's life, then you would be enlightened by reading some (or all) of the stirring memoirs chronicled in *Mentors, Masters and Mrs. MacGregor—Stories of Teachers Making a Difference,* by author Jane Bluestein, Ph.D. Her delightful book features interviews with more than 170 individuals and celebrities from varied walks of life, whose lives were profoundly touched by a teacher or mentor.

Bluestein shares the following conclusion:

If I had any doubts before I started this book, I am now entirely convinced that we do indeed touch one another's lives. We are products of a lifetime of experiences, events, interactions, a word or a look—any of which can have a profound effect on who or what we become in life.

How we act with one another matters because people notice and they remember, and they sometimes carry these memories throughout their lives. It reassures me to know no matter how many negative forces are at work in a person's life, it often takes no more than one person, one act of love or acceptance or encouragement, to make a difference.

More often than not, that person will never see, nor receive evidence of the impact he or she has had on us—unless we stop and say, "Thanks for making a difference in my life!"

Encouragement: How To Spread It

When people ask me about my children, or how many I have, one of my favorite responses goes like this:

"Well, I will say that before I had any children, I had six strongly-held theories about how I would raise my kids. But, now that I have six children of my own, I have no more theories."

While this remark often brings a chuckle from kindred parents—it's not entirely accurate. Yes, I have six children, but to claim as a result that I have "no more theories" is not true.

My father passed away over a decade ago. At his memorial service, I shared in tears that I would miss my favorite cheerleader. Especially his, "what's awesome about you" stories. He seemed to love to share short tales chronicling something I achieved—an award or some obstacle or difficulty I overcame—and he repeated them often. I'm only slightly embarrassed to say I enjoyed them more and more on the retelling.

Of course, he had "awesome you" stories about each of my brothers and sisters. It was one of his more endearing ways of sharing his love—and a gift that sustains me still today.

(After the memorial, one of my close friends shared, "You're so fortunate. My dad preferred to talk about whatever he thought I was doing wrong.")

So now I have this firmly held fathering theory: all children need guidance, counsel, and love. They need leadership and good character, especially when modeled by example. And one of the easiest ways to show your love is by freely sharing their "awesome you" stories.

Thank you, Dad!

How To Develop "Awesome You" Stories

Here's a question: who do you know that wouldn't enjoy some heartfelt encouragement?

Here's the answer: everyone you know!

(If you're a baby-boomer, buy a set of large notecards. If you're from a younger generation adapt these instructions to your favorite digital app to record your notes.)

Begin by putting the name of each of your children at the top of a separate card. Add your spouse's name to another card. Brothers, sisters, Mom, Dad—add their names to separate cards or pages. You decide how many "awesome you" people stories you want to create and share.

On each, write a note or record a sentence or phrase that reminds you, or prompts you to share a story about a time when that person did "something awesome." It can be something large or small, such as simple kindness they did for you or someone else or any obstacle they overcame. What is it about their unique personality, or values, or character that are admirable? How is this person a "difference maker"?

"Awesome you" stories deliver more benefits than praise. These stories lift other's spirits. They help remind us that there are exceptional people in the world doing good things, overcoming difficulties, and breaking through barriers.

My good friend Larry Weeks often shares "awesome you" stories when he is introducing two or more people. It's a much better conversation starter than complaining about the weather, and it's an endearing quality Larry usually begins with, "Do you know what's amazing about Sue?" Or, "Do you know what Bill does so well?" "Did I ever tell you about the time that Monte …?"

Seek To Find Another's "O"

Let me explain.

There's a revealing story about a frustrated teacher who begged Dr. Dreikurs to tell her how she might be able to "finally get through" to one of her most challenging students. She handed the doctor a sample of her pupil's homework and complained, "Look at this appalling handwriting!"

Dreikurs studied the paper very carefully, turning it sideways and upside down. After a few minutes, he commented, "Hmmm… look at the perfect circular o in this writing. Did you notice how symmetrical they are?"

"What are you saying?" the incredulous teacher asked.

"The o," Driekurs responded. "Every o is beautiful. Don't you agree?"

Of course, Driekurs was trying to help the teacher recognize "at least one beautiful thing" about her student's handwriting. She needed to discover a bridge to connection and encouragement for her student.

One of the chief characteristics of an encourager is the willingness to recognize and acknowledge even the slightest "o" in others. The delightfully complex, ongoing process of

101

interacting with others in harmony is one of the more intriguing peculiarities about human behavior—yet one of the most rewarding. "Able encouragers " soon learn that the more you invest in someone else's positive experience, the more blessings you bring to your own experiences.

The simple truth is we all need each other.

There is an old fable that tells the story of a young girl who is walking through a field when she sees a butterfly stuck on a thorn. She releases the butterfly carefully, and it suddenly transforms into a good fairy that tells the girl, "Because of your kindness I will grant you your fondest wish."

Thinking for a moment, the little girl responds, "I just want to be happy." So the fairy leans in and whispers in the girl's ear— and then vanishes.

As she grew older, there was no one in the land happier than the girl. If someone asked the girl for the secret of her happiness, she would always smile and say, "I just listened to a good fairy."

When she grew quite old, the people of the land were afraid the girl's secret might die with her. Please tell us," they begged. "Tell us what the fairy said."

Eventually, the now lovely old lady smiled and answered, "The fairy said that everyone, no matter how secure they seemed, still had great need of me!"

The simple truth is that we all need encouragers!

Sample Statements That Spread Encouragement

Words have the marvelous capacity to uplift and to bring transformation, and to change lives. They have the uncanny power to make living things die—or bring dead things to life.

Here are a few sample encouragement statements that will help get you started. Remember too, it's not what you say, but what people feel when you say them. Your sincere and authentic intention to uplift another's spirit is much more important than the precise words. Once your purpose is clear, you will discover you have exactly the right words to say, and in your unique style of expression.

While gratitude, empathy, and compassion can be legitimately communicated non-verbally with emotion, encouragement, on the other hand, benefits greatly from its *oral expression.*

Encouraging Statements For Meetings and Business

At a board meeting or any group meeting, before moving on to the next agenda item, stop to thank and give credit to those who made a suggestion, or contributed in any way, even if their contribution created an unexpected debate or deliberations.

Applaud the wisdom or insight of a suggestion someone offered.

> "Thanks for giving us more ideas to consider before we make a decision."

> "Thanks for helping us flesh out the important details."

> "Thanks for helping us deliberate more carefully on that issue."

> "You helped us with some points we might have missed. Thank you."

> "Your contribution was very beneficial."

"Your insights made a big difference to the quality of our thinking."

"Thanks for being here and lending your support; it means so much."

"You've been very generous with your suggestions and your time."

"Our chief want is someone who will inspire us to be what we know we could be." —Ralph Waldo Emerson

You Inspired Me Statements For Cards, Letters and In-Person

Write enthusiastic and encouraging notes to people. Hint: children love notes too. It is almost impossible to calculate the lasting effect of positive encouragement offered to a child. Write a personal letter or note card that a friend or an employee can take home or put in a personnel file. Keep a supply of blank note cards in your desk for exactly that purpose.

Tell someone specifically what it is they do (or did) that inspires you in some way.

"You probably don't know this, but you inspire me to be a kinder person."

"I am so proud of the (person, man, woman) you've become."

"I admire your never-ending selfless love for your children and family."

"I admire your tenacity and courage! It encourages me to stay focused and strong."

"Your beauty and personality are so unique!"

"I love how you love the forgotten and care for the afflicted. You make me want to pay better attention to people that need my help."

"You never seem to give up even when things are difficult or uncertain. I want to learn that from you."

"For the rest of his life, Oliver Twist remembers a single word of blessing spoken to him by another child because this word stood out so strikingly from the consistent discouragement around him." –Charles Dickens, Oliver Twist

Statements That Show You Notice: The Little Things Matter

Because we expect them, we don't typically praise essential services such as bussing the dishes in restaurants, mopping the restroom floor, filling the paper towel holders in public common areas. Be the person who notices the hard workers who serve you and others behind the scenes.

"You do such an outstanding job for all of us."

"I hope you know what an important difference you make."

"You are so careful and considerate."

"I wanted you to know that I notice, and so do others."

"That looks like a tough job. Thank you for doing it so cheerfully."

"Encouragement from any source is like a drop of rain upon a parched desert. Thanks to all the many others who rained on

me when I needed it, and even when I foolishly thought I didn't. —Claire Gillian

Encourage Positive Qualities And Character

Commend them for the kindness, compassion or sensitivity with which he or she treated another person. You noticed, and so does the universe.

Push yourself daily, to affirm another person's existence. Get up from your chair, seek out someone, and say, "I just came by to say hello," or "good morning."

Pick up the phone and say, "I called to tell you how much I appreciate you," or, "I called to say thank you for the contributions you make."

"What I am thankful for about you, is …"

"What I appreciate so much about you is …"

"What inspires me about you is …"

"What I've learned from you is …"

"Your willingness to be a good friend to people you care about inspires me to be a better friend to all the people I love."

"You help make me be a better person because…"

"The way you handled that situation inspired me to …"

Encouraging Statements For Teachers and Educators

"You've been working very hard on your math problems. Keep up the good job because I know you're going to do well on your tests."

"Your project was very detailed and well planned. Have you ever considered a career in science?"

"I don't know if you've thought of grad school before, but I believe that you're capable of exceeding as a grad student."

"Your drawings are so interesting and beautiful, have you thought about a career in design?"

"I'm so impressed with how much your writing has improved; I believe that you could be an author someday."

"You have such a natural feel for music; you could have a career as a musician. Oh, and be sure and have a backup plan or you might starve." (Monte Sr. to me when I was about 12 years old.)

"I liked what I saw from you in class today; it tells me that you are ..."

"Wow, you are getting to where you need to be. Keep it going!"

"It is not easy to ... but, you are making it happen."

"Instruction does much, but encouragement everything."
—Johann Wolfgang von Goethe

Ask For Someone's Advice. Listen Quietly and Intently.

"I'd greatly appreciate your perspective on this."

"Would you be willing to offer your assessment of something?"

"I'd be so grateful for your opinion."

"I need your advice on something that is very important to me."

"I need the unique brand of expertise that you bring to the table."

"Treat a man as he is and he will remain as he is. Treat a man as he can and should be, and he will become as he can and should be." —Stephen R. Covey

Encourage Someone Who Is Hurting

If you want to offer help to someone who is experiencing emotional or physical pain, it's important to stay focused on your intention to help them by being there, and not be there to make yourself feel good about yourself for doing good.

It's not necessary for you to have all the answers or the solutions to their issues. By being (1) gently present, (2) kind, and (3) compassionate, you are demonstrating three of the most powerful way to help someone who is suffering.

"I see, hear and love," are three potent phrases of compassionate encouragement. This powerful heart language serves to help the person feel seen, heard, and loved.

"I see (the pain or challenge) you are experiencing."

"I hear you."

"I don't know what to say, but I'm here for you."

I'll never forget a time when I was experiencing deep emotional pain from the breakup of a relationship with someone who had been in my life for many years. My amazing wife walked up to me and put her arms around me for what seemed like twenty minutes. There was nothing she could say or needed to say. She was simply "there for me."

Our deepest longings are found in being seen, known, and loved. Choose to see and empathize with the other person for what they are experiencing. Listen as they work through the painful emotions, and decide to love them in the midst of it all.

"No matter how much suffering you may go through, you may never want to let go of those memories." — *Haruki Murakami*

The habitude of encouragement is an extraordinary heart language gift that can ignite the spirit and communicate your faith in another.

When you encourage others, you boost their self-esteem, enhance their self-confidence, lift their spirits and help make it possible for them to succeed. It is unquestionably one of the most powerful ways through which you can express support and love for another human being.

Like the waves you create by tossing a pebble in a pond, encouragement not only impacts the person you encouraged but can also spread to the people they touch, their children, their spouse, and generations of family for years to come.

Be an encourager.

Spread encouragement generously!

CHAPTER FIVE

The Habitude of Leaking Joy

"Misery is easy, Syracuse. Happiness you have to work at." – Ondine

How To Quickly Win The Hearts of Millions

I don't believe there is any Facebook, Instagram, Twitter, or "fan-harvesting" social media app nearly as effective for creating followers as the clever scheme employed by Roberta Vinci.

Vinci is the Italian tennis player who, against estimated 300:1 odds, defeated Serena Williams in the semifinals of the 2015 U.S. open. Media outlets described Roberta's win as one of the biggest upsets in tennis history.

"It's like a dream," said Roberta, who at 32 years, six months, became the oldest first-time Grand Slam finalist in the open era. "I'm really happy, but of course, I'm a little bit sad for Serena because she's an incredible player…"

The lesson to be learned from her win is *not* about Vinci's evident grit, determination, resilience or sportsmanship, nor is it a David and Goliath sports fable.

The real story emerges when we recognize the powerful, age-old method Vinci used to capture the hearts and minds of millions of fans, press and media broadcasters, and how she managed to enchant many of the often fickle New York tennis onlookers during one weekend in September.

How did she do it?

She leaked her joy. During (and after) her match, Vinci committed repeated acts of sheer, unmitigated, in-your-face joy. Roberta was blatantly thrilled to be part of the game, to be in New York, on center court, in front of thousands of fans, competing against superstar Serena Williams. She was shamelessly elated during both her pre- and post-match interviews.

Like a wide-eyed three-year-old on Christmas morning, somehow so grateful for the bows, boxes, and wrapping paper, she could care less what was inside. Vinci was relentless. She kept leaking her joy.

And then she somehow "accidentally won"!

The very next day, after losing the tournament final to her good friend, Flavia Panetta, instead of the obligatory after-match handshake we've come to expect, Vinci hugged Flavia tight for nearly a minute, whispering congratulations.

If you'd happened to turn on your TV at that moment, it would have been difficult for you to determine which player won the match. In the awards presentation ceremony, Vinci turned on her 10,000-watt grin, held her runner-up plate for all to see—thankful, grateful, jubilant, and giving all the credit to the fans, the sponsors, and especially to Flavia.

Her joyful spirit leaked out and spread everywhere—bringing many of the audience to tears. I know, because her performance brought me to tears.

Joyful, joyful, joyful!

There are important heart language lessons available from studying Roberta Vinci's behavior. There are leadership lessons, the law of attraction lessons, and life lessons—if you are willing to take notice and change your "joy paradigm."

Joy might be, in fact, not only something to enjoy, but also a heart-language habitude that can help each of us see life much more clearly. In and of itself joy may be one of the most powerful life-lessons of all.

In both life and tennis, you can't always control what's going on across the net from you. Sometimes you win, and sometimes you lose. But if you want to inspire people, empower and influence others, perhaps thousands of others, then in every moment possible, find a way to leak your joy—and spread it everywhere—unreservedly.

That's called winning at life.

Joy is very, very, attractive. It creates fans and goodwill better than any app you'll ever find, anywhere.

Choosing Joy Even When It's Hard

There is an eloquent short verse penned by Samuel Ullman, a nineteenth-century poet who wrote, "Years may wrinkle the skin, but to give up enthusiasm wrinkles the soul."

It's a tender comment—and a valuable warning—about what can happen if you lose your joy. If at any age, or any time of your life, you choose to let go of your passion or zest for living. After all, who wants a wrinkled soul?

But what if bad things happen that you didn't choose? How about something awful? Is it possible to still choose joy?

Jim -the head coach at North Carolina State University who won the 1983 NCAA basketball tournament against very long odds. Valvano was not only known for running up and down the court after winning the championship, seemingly in disbelief, looking for someone to hug, but he's also known for the inspirational 1993 Espy award speech he gave weeks before he died.

A few months earlier, in June 1992, Valvano was diagnosed with a fast moving, invasive and lethal type of bone cancer. While he was accepting the inaugural Arthur Ashe Courage and Humanitarian Award, the teleprompter blinked that Jim had just 30 seconds remaining to speak.

Valvano responded:

"They've got that screen up there flashing "30-seconds left"! Like I care about that screen. I've got tumors all over my body, and I'm worried about some guy in the back going thirty seconds." He laughed, and so did the audience. And his speech included these recommendations to the listeners:

"To me, there are three things we all should do every day. We should do these every day of our lives.

"Number one is to laugh. You should laugh every day."

And while Valvano didn't cite any evidence for his advice, the skeptics among us should know that there are studies that link—if not prove—that laughter is good for the heart. Really good! And not only the heart but also the whole body, the mind, and perhaps even the soul.

It's revealing that the Navajo Indians have a tradition where they celebrate a baby's first laugh as a rite of passage—a moment in which the Navajo baby laughs at himself and begins the first move into "baby-dom" and conscious humanity. Why not? Laughter feels good. It's like fabric softener for the soul.

"And number two," Valvano continued:

"Think. You should spend time every day in thought."

He didn't elaborate, but I believe most of the listeners understood. I choose to believe that Valvano was reminding us to pause a moment each day and ask ourselves, "What's important? What should I pay attention to in my life that matters?" Maybe before we spend years chasing success, we should spend a few precious minutes thinking about it and defining it.

Maybe we should spend time hugging the people we care about the most. And maybe we should spend more time talking about things that matter with people we care about instead of wasting our time talking about things that don't matter with people we don't care about.

Of course, each of us must decide what matters most.

"And number three," he said:

"You should have your emotions moved to tears every day … could be tears of happiness or joy. But think about it. If you laugh, you think, and you cry, that's a full day. That's a heck of a day. You do that seven days a week, and you're going to have something special."

Although he was near the very end of his life's journey, Valvano's unbending joy never seemed to diminish. He, as

Samuel Ullman before him, understood that to give up joy wrinkles the soul.

Valvano closed by saying:

"Cancer can take away all my physical abilities. It cannot touch my mind, it cannot touch my heart, and it cannot touch my soul. And those three things are going to carry on forever."

Profound advice from a man who had nothing to lose: laugh each day. Take a moment for some real thought. Let your emotions soar. Happiness, joy, even tears. It doesn't matter.

Jim Valvano received a standing ovation from the crowd. His memorable acceptance speech became legendary.

No wrinkled souls allowed.

The Science of Joy

Researcher and University of Wisconsin professor of psychology, Richard Davidson, claims, "Happiness isn't this vague, ineffable feeling; it's a physical state of the brain—one that you can induce deliberately."

Moreover, emotions of joy and happiness have a powerful influence on the rest of the body. People who rate on the higher end of the happiness scale in psychological tests develop 50% more antibodies than average in response to flu vaccines. That, says Davidson, is an enormous difference.

According to a nine-year Dutch study of elderly patients, upbeat mental states of joy, happiness, and optimism reduced or limited the risk of cardiovascular disease, diabetes, hypertension, colds, and upper respiratory infections. Surprisingly, these states reduced the participant's risk of death by 50% over the study's nine-year duration.

Harvard School of Public Health psychologist, Laura Kubzansky noted, "There are measurable positive benefits of joy, happiness, and optimism." In a separate study, Kubzansky tracked 1300 men for ten years and found that heart disease rates among men who called themselves "generally happy and optimistic" were half the disease rates of those who didn't.

With our increasing ability to accurately measure physiological changes in the body, scientists have discovered that "happy, hopeful, optimists" have lower levels of cortisol, the hormone produced by the adrenal gland in response to stress. Cortisol is known to reduce immune function.

Joy, optimism, and hopefulness appear to help people feel less stress and seemingly help people avoid the noxious biochemical cascades that high stress is known to trigger.

Leading-edge cellular biologist and author, Bruce Lipton, makes a compelling case for "finding our joy." Lipton claims that our attitudes and beliefs impact each of us not only on a cellular level but also on a genetic level:

"Positive thoughts have a profound effect on behavior and genes … and negative thoughts have an equally powerful effect. When we recognize how these positive and negative beliefs control our biology, we can use this knowledge to create lives filled with health and happiness."

Feelings of joy, happiness, and well-being are worthwhile habitudes to pursue, not only for oneself, but for the people you touch. Research shows that expressing these emotions also positively influences the emotions of those around us—up to three levels of separation. Albert Schweitzer, the German physician and Nobel Peace Prize winner was right when he said, "Happiness is the only thing that multiplies when you share it."

Scientists such as Lipton, claim we carry a field of energy around us that interacts with the energy field of others. This "aura" can radiate conflict and anger—or joy, harmony, and serenity. We radiate what we feel. We radiate what we are. Could this be, in part, why when joyful, outgoing people enter a room, everyone else is suddenly in a better mood?

In addition to your emotion's ability to impact, attract and even repel others, one of the most fascinating and growing areas of science, known as epigenetics, (meaning "above genetics") demonstrates that emotions do in fact impact the body on a cellular level. Environmental influences, including nutrition, stress, *and emotions*, can modify our genes without changing their basic blueprint and measurably affect our health positively or negatively.

Ever since Norman Cousins cured himself of ankylosing spondylitis (a painful inflammatory condition) by watching Marx Brothers' videos, research on the healing effects of joy, happiness, and humor has flourished. Researchers have learned, for example, that humor strengthens the immune system, lowers blood pressure and reduces stress.

In his groundbreaking book, *The Biology of Belief*, Lipton notes:

"Biological behavior can be controlled by invisible forces, including thought, as well as it can be controlled by physical molecules like penicillin, a fact that provides the scientific underpinning for pharmaceutical-free energy medicine."

A wave of new research based on the concept of "positive psychology" has drawn attention to the study of the effects of qualities, such as optimism versus pessimism. A patient study conducted at the Mayo Clinic indicated that of 839 subjects tested 30 years earlier, those individuals categorized as pessimists had a 40% greater probability of dying than those classified as optimists.

"It confirmed our common-sense belief," says Dr. Maruta of the Mayo Clinic. "It tells us that mind and body are linked, and that attitude has an impact on the ultimate outcome— death." Simply stated, the researcher noted, "An optimistic outlook on life could result in a longer and healthier life."

Gloom and doom could also increase the risk of death from heart disease. Finnish researchers followed 2,267 middle-aged and older men and women for 11 years and evaluated their outlook on life. They discovered that those who scored high on the pessimism scale were more than twice as likely to die of heart disease versus those who ranked lowest. We don't know yet why this association exists, but researchers suggest, "Pessimism may increase inflammation and other factors that negatively affect heart health."

Dr. Lipton offers the following explanation:

"The practical (and spiritual) eureka moment is when I realized that the cell membrane is a liquid crystal semiconductor with gates and channels. And like our computer, our cells are utterly programmable by our environment, *our thoughts AND our beliefs*."

"We are the drivers of our personal biology, just as I am the driver of this word processing program. We have the ability to edit the data we enter into our biocomputers, just as surely as I can choose the words I type."

"You need more than just positive thinking to harness control of your body and your life. It is important for our health and well-being to shift our mind's energy towards positive, life-generating thoughts and eliminate ever-present, energy-draining, and debilitating negative thoughts."

While it's heartening to know there is tremendous objective evidence to support the positive effects of joy, I'll close this section with a quote by the wonderful Piero Ferrucci, a leading transpersonal psychologist and author of *The Power of Kindness,* who offered this about joy:

"We do not need research to know that joy feels great. The question is, how do we go about it?"

Great question!

Misery Is Easy—Joy Takes Practice

It's revealing to note that most of us think of joy and happiness as something we need to pursue—or find—yet research now suggests otherwise. It turns out that even joy and happiness aren't as elusive as some people believe.

In fact joy, happiness, and gratitude—if we learn how to practice them—are developable habits (habitudes) we can begin to cultivate and experience to a greater degree.

Leading neuroscientists now claim that we can teach ourselves how to be happy, more joyful, and more grateful. And, no different than learning to play the piano or learning to engage in a complicated sport—we have to practice.

Joy Exercises That Work

Begin with the acceptance that joy is our natural state. Joy is not an abstract concept, but the way we were meant to be. By acknowledging that joy is natural, and by saying, "I welcome more joy in my life," your affirmation begins to set in motion the emotional and physiological changes you desire.

Dr. Wayne Dyer reminded us that all emotions are physical manifestations of our thoughts:

> Yes, you can create miracles for yourself through the magical use of your mind. Our thoughts produce physical manifestations that we have learned to call emotions.
>
> The molecules that make up the emotions derive directly from your mental world. The joy you experience is located in your physical body and the chemicals that are present when you experience elation can be identified and quantified.
>
> The same goes for fear, stress, anger, rage, jealousy, phobic reactions and the like. These are all chemical changes that are taking place within you. You manufacture those chemicals in your private quantum pharmacy, the process begins with your mind. The mind is capable of manufacturing—from scratch—the thousands of "drugs" that show up in your body. You need not necessarily go to the drug store. Your mind can create what your body needs.

Mounting evidence from numerous clinical trials and evaluative studies demonstrates that the "placebo effect" (the positive effect of a harmless or inert substance apparently due to the subject's belief that he or she is taking a real drug or receiving an actual surgical or medical procedure). In many cases, the placebo is as powerful, or more powerful than the drugs it is used to measure.

For example, a Baylor School of Medicine study, published in 2002 in the New England Journal of Medicine evaluated surgery for patients with severe, debilitating knee pain. (Moseley, et al., 2002) The results were extraordinary: the group who received surgery improved, as expected. But the placebo group improved as much as the other group! Despite the fact that there are over 600,000 surgeries yearly for arthritic knees, the study results demonstrated that the entire benefit of surgery for osteoarthritis of the knee was the placebo effect.

Another rigorous evaluative study found that 80% of the effect of antidepressants, as measured in clinical trials, could be attributed to the placebo effect. The data revealed that in more than half of the clinical trials for the six leading antidepressants, the drugs did not outperform the placebo— sugar pills.

Additional studies have shown the placebo effect to be equally as potent in treating diseases such as asthma and Parkinson's; even when subjects know they're not getting a drug, the placebo pills still work.

Suffice to say that your mind is incredibly powerful. The problem with most of us is that we've restricted ourselves to only a few choices of our available emotional realm. We believe that joy is not sustainable, or that continually expressing joy puts the spotlight on us and somehow takes something away from others.

Affirm Your Intention To Welcome More Joy In Your Life.

The secret to changing your life is realizing this: your intention creates your reality. Wishing, hoping, and goal-setting cannot accomplish change without specific intention. Do not underestimate the power of your mind or the power of intention to help you manifest and create the joy you want to bring into your life. Oprah Winfrey repeatedly declares, "Intention rules the universe."

In a few minutes, perhaps as you awaken, and once again right before you close your eyes, you can say or silently affirm: *"Every day, and in every way, I welcome more and more joy into my life."*

As Wayne Dyer so eloquently stated, "Intention is the energy of your soul coming in contact with your physical reality."

To Experience More Joy—Spread Joy By Way of Gratitude

As we discovered in Chapter One, the practice of affirming the goodness in one's life fosters positive chemical changes in the brain—and perhaps throughout the entire body.

We also know, through many scientific studies, that the "emotion of gratitude" is increasingly linked with improved human health, and the "practice of gratitude" helps lower stress, depression, and appears to reduce a host of reported physical symptoms.

It may not surprise you to know that the act of demonstrating gratitude not only improves our ability to connect with others but also engenders tremendous feelings of joy and happiness in the person expressing it.

Know this: Expressing your gratitude to others is an outrageously effective way to create more joy in your life; it's the ultimate example of "give and receive."

Want to give your body and mind a "quick and healthy joy fix"? Call someone you are close to and sincerely express why you are grateful to have them in your life.

Go ahead and "leak your joy." Joy is a feeling that's available to you no matter what else is going on in your life. It's one of the easiest feelings to produce. You need only remember to take a moment to create it.

Your Inner Divining Rod To Joy

One theory of life, the "hedonistic theory" claims that joy and happiness occur when pleasure is at an absolute maximum. The "eudaemonistic theory" of life holds that we are the happiest when we discover its meaning. In other words, what counts most is what we believe. Joy comes when (and because) our life has purpose and meaning.

The oddest question Val Van De Wall ever asked me, or at least I thought so at the time, was, "Monte, what's your purpose in life?"

I don't remember exactly how I responded, but whatever it was made Val snicker and say, "No, I don't think that's it." After almost ten minutes of my lobbying a variety of off-the-cuff ideas about my life's purpose, about all I could elicit from Val was a warm chuckle, "Nope", or "Nice try."

For nearly a year I continued to reflect on my purpose and then phone Val to run it by him. My "eureka purpose moment" finally arrived. I was sitting in my car in the parking lot of a small shopping center in Altamonte Springs, Florida. I scribbled it down and phoned Val in Canada to share this:

"I'm a joyful teacher and coach. My purpose is to lift myself and others to new possibilities in life, to our highest and best futures. (The remainder I leave out here because I believe one's full purpose is private and personal. Think of it as a beautiful plant. Keep the roots, and the essence of it secure within yourself, but let the world share in its fruits.)

Val was quiet for a moment, and then asked, "Does that wiggle your brain cells like it does mine?"

"Absolutely," I said.

"Congratulations," he offered.

And I could feel a hair-raising-on-the-back-of-my-neck sense of joy, elation, and serenity, and not because of his approval. I knew my purpose was right on target (for me) even before I called. That was over 25 years ago, and that conversation with Val remains vibrant and vivid in my memory.

I've changed only one word of "Monte's purpose" over the ensuing years. Now it begins, "I'm a joyful teacher, author, and coach ..."

My friend and colleague, Bill Cortright, in his extraordinary best-selling book, *The New Stress Response Diet and Lifestyle Program: A Total Metabolic Reset*, shares the story of his personal transformation from a life impaired by the pain of obesity—to his current life as a world-class fitness scientist. Bill is an author, coach, life trainer and popular speaker, who has helped thousands of people get motivated, get fit, reduce the need for medications, and ultimately regain their health.

Bill talks passionately about, "tapping into a force that will change you and your life forever ... and when you do—everything you do seems so effortless and is sheer pleasure."

Bill writes:

> The main thing you need to tap into this power on a regular basis is a *defined purpose for your life*. I did find my purpose over 20 years ago, And, I base everything I do on that definition.
>
> My purpose is to motivate, educate, and inspire people to live a healthy and balanced life. How does this work in my life?
>
> I go to work every single day and do what I love. The way I accomplished this was to create my job, my business and

my career based on my purpose. I am here to live in each moment of each day.

If I can keep 100 pounds off for 33 years, anyone can.

A sense of purpose can not only help you lose weight, it can help you sleep: A new study in Sleep Science and Practice found that people who reported having a strong sense of purpose were 63% less likely to have sleep apnea and 52% less likely to have restless leg syndrome than those who scored lower on the purpose scale.

I've reviewed many "Find your purpose" exercises over time. This one, from authors John-Roger and Peter McWilliams, is one of my favorites, and the one I employed over 25 years ago:

What is your purpose?

> A purpose is something you discover. It's already there. It's always been there. You've lived your life by it, perhaps without fully realizing it. (Although when you do discover it, you will know that you've known it all along.)
>
> A purpose is not a goal. A goal is something that you can reach. A purpose is a direction, like East. No matter how far east you go, there is still more east to travel.
>
> A purpose is never achieved; it is fulfilled in each moment that you are "on purpose." You use your purpose to set your course in life. When you are "on course," you are "on purpose." You have always had a purpose. It has always been the same purpose. Your purpose will—for the remainder of this lifetime, at least—remain the same.
>
> 1. Make a list of all your positive qualities. (This is not the time for modesty. False humility, by the way, is just a form of egoism.) Narrow down each of your good qualities to one or two words. "Loving, giving, joyful, playful, loyal, tender, caring, etc." Write them down. If your list is short, ask

friends for their suggestions. Use these words as a starting point. Find the two or three that suit you best, and arrange them in a sentence starting with, "I..." or "I am..." When you discover your purpose, it will click immediately.

2. On another page, start listing actions you find nurturing. List the positive things you like doing most. Giving? Sharing? Teaching? Learning? Take some time with this process. Reflect upon your life. Explore its motivation. Ask yourself, "What activities give me the most satisfaction?"

If you get stuck, call a few friends and ask them, "What are my best qualities?"

Consider the people you admire most. What is that you admire most about them? What qualities do they embody? Those same qualities are likely true about you too, so write them down.

Eventually, a pattern will emerge on the qualities and actions list. The idea is not to discover which qualities and action patterns are "right" but which of these qualities resonate most clearly within you.

3. Before going to sleep, give yourself the instruction, "When I wake up in the morning, I will know my purpose." Have a pen and paper by your bed and, first thing when you wake up, write whatever words are there.

Your discovery may come with equal parts of joy and resignation: Joy at seeing that your life has had a direction all along; resignation in noticing it may not be quite as glamorous as you had secretly hoped.

Nevertheless, that's your purpose!

So does defining your purpose bring constant joy to your life? Not necessarily, but "discovering your purpose" is an important touchstone for your life's direction; it is your private and innermost divining rod of truth.

Garvin DeShazer, my colleague, friend, and author of *Lovin' Life—A Guide To Authentic Self-Discovery*, offers these intriguing questions about the importance of finding joy through purpose:

> 1. Where can I express my gifts in a way that brings the deep satisfaction of knowing I am in alignment with my purpose?
>
> 2. I don't have to look far, do I? Who in my family? Who in my circle of close friends? Who amongst my acquaintances? Who at my workplace? Who at my church, temple or mosque? Who within the organizations of my community that I have yet to meet?
>
> 3. Am I ready to begin fulfilling my purpose in life?
>
> 4. Am I ready to claim and fully own the truth that I am a special, unique and magnificent expression of Divine creative love?
>
> 5. Am I ready to know how it feels to be filled with a deep, abiding joy?
>
> 6. Am I ready to be an Agent of Love in the world?
>
> 7. What am I waiting for?

In your lifetime you will have many debates with yourself about what to do; numerous self-conversations about what direction to take. Most of these debates will be resolved by asking, "What is the choice that will keep me on purpose?" Then go in that direction one step at a time.

The benefit of knowing you carry a "trustworthy inner guidance system" you can always count on is as close to joy as anything else you can experience.

ARK To Create Joy

There's a beautiful old Eastern story, shared by Piero Ferrucci, in his marvelous book, *The Power of Kindness*.

> God wants to reward a man for his exceptional kindness and purity of intentions. He calls an angel and tells him to go to the man and ask him what he wants. He will give the man whatever his heart desires. The angel appears before the kind man and gives him the good news. The man replies, "Oh, but I am already happy. I have all that I want." The angel explains that, with God, you must be very tactful. If He wants to give you a gift, it is best to accept. The kind man then replies, "In this case, I would like all who come in contact with me to feel well. But I want to know nothing about it."
>
> From that moment, wherever the kind man happens to be, wilted plants bloom again, sickly animals grow strong, ill people are healed, the unhappy are relieved of their burdens, those who fight make peace, and those beset by problems resolve them. And all this happens without the kind man knowing—always in his wake, but never in front of his eyes. There is never any pride, nor any expectation. Unknowing and content, the kindly man walks the roads of the world, spreading happiness to everybody.

A study by Canadian psychologists says we are hardwired to appreciate others' happiness. The researchers claim that personal joy can be created easily by being nice—not so much by being respectful or polite, but by bringing out the joy and goodness of others through acts of kindness.

Especially compelling are the unexpected "acts of random kindness." (Hence the acronym "ARK") One of the study's authors, Lynn Alden, a professor of psychology at the University of British Columbia says, "It's about being alert for things you can do spontaneously for other people—because you want to. The good news is that it has the side effect of making you feel good," she explains.

129

In her new book, *The How of Happiness*, University Professor Dr. Sonja Lyubomirsky argues that much of our happiness "is about intentional activities that we can choose to engage in—those things that we can do every day of our lives."

Dr. Richard Davidson at the University of Wisconsin research data shows that if a person sits quietly for a half-hour a day thinking about compassion and kindness, their brain will show noticeable changes in two weeks.

"In many ways, this is the most important idea in neuroscience in the last decade," he says. "Our brains are eager and waiting to be transformed, and they're always being transformed. Now we know we can take responsibility and change our brain in more positive ways.

Lyubomirsky adds, "The research shows happiness is undeniably within us—not outside of us. It's in what we do and how we act."

Scientists know that happy people practice more acts of kindness, avoid dwelling on their problems, and can lose themselves in whatever they are doing.

Life-Life Balance Creates More Joy

When we think of the word "balance", perhaps we first think about balance in nature, athletics or the creative arts. A different type of balance, work-life, is the subject of an ongoing debate among business professionals who seek the answer to the question: "How do I reconcile my personal and professional lives?" Weighing in, a Harvard Business School survey of almost 4000 executives concluded: "Work-life balance is an elusive ideal and at worst a complete myth."

My first thought after reading the study result was, any survey using the term "work-life" creates a bias that suggests that "work" and "life" are naturally at odds with each other; two contradictory goals that clash with one's natural happiness. Next, I wondered: if the Harvard study conclusion holds water, then why should anyone waste time seeking work-life balance?

Good question! What if, instead, we consider the concept of "life-life" balance?

Psychologists suggest that when one area of a person's life is distressed, there's a natural tendency for people to measure their overall quality of life through the lens of the single troubled area. For example, a person may be in excellent physical shape, have an outstanding professional career, enjoy a large circle of friends, but when his or her significant other relationship is suffering, they feel overall, "life sucks."

My dear friend, Lisa Broesh-Weeks, the talented life coach, speaker, and author of *Practical Bliss — The Busy Person's Guide To Happiness* suggests that life-balance doesn't have to be perfect, but we should invest wisely if we want high returns from our life-balance decisions:

> I like to think of the concept of time as if it were a bank balance, with the option to use every second to either invest in your future or frivolously spend with no expected return.
>
> You can make deposits by investing your time in meaningful projects, education, relationship building, improving your health, and anything else that may bring you a "return." Or you can spend your time on the optional obligations and stressors that bring you down, wear you out, and have little or nothing to do with the intention/vision you have for your life. In that case, you're not banking anything. You're frittering away your time without investing

it, and at the end of the page, you don't have an equal return.

When it comes to Living in Bliss, you're going to need to find room in your days, weeks, and months to include the events and things that truly make you feel good, and weed out the stuff that doesn't.

The simple truth is that the decisions we make in any area of our lives tend to impact and influence all other areas. The quality of our personal relationships affects our professional and business lives. Financial health can affect our physical and mental health and. One's energy level, fitness, mental, spiritual, and physical health touch all other areas.

It would be a strong person indeed who was willing to say, "Although I'm dying of brain cancer, all things being equal, my overall quality of life is fantastic."

Dr. Joe Vitale has a simple but effective method for helping people determine where their life is "out of balance." It's as simple as asking yourself "What am I complaining about the most?" When you answer the question honestly, it's an important clue to where your life is out of balance.

Vitale offers what he calls his "Million Dollar" technique for getting what you want. (Balance)

Know what you don't want (What is it you complain about the most?)

Select what you do want in its place (Set your intention).

Clean out any interference that's between you and your intention (Fear, indecision, laziness).

Visualize what it would feel like to have what you want (your intention). Imagine that it has already come to pass.

Completely let go of any anxiety, desperation or fear about your ability to realize your intention. Keep affirming, "Everything is unfolding the way I want."

Leaking Joy: In Conclusion

There is no easy answer to the question of finding life-life balance. Your personal "balance points" are always shifting and changing. When you notice an out-of-balance area of your life, take steps to put it back in balance.

Of course, there are other reasons to continue to strive for life-life balance, but added joy is one of the greatest benefits. The simple and uncomplicated act of *beginning* to put your life back in balance brings more joy.

People often report *by merely creating the intention and taking the initial steps* it immediately increases their level of joy and happiness. In other words, you don't have to have achieved the balance to begin experiencing more joy.

How? — Take the small steps. Forgive yourself, and everyone and everything that may have contributed to limiting your joy in the past. Joy can still be part of you regardless of anything else you are feeling, thinking and doing. The past is the past.

When? — Begin now. Here's the secret: Deciding to love yourself brings more joy. Seeking balance in your life is a tremendous step towards demonstrating your love for yourself—to yourself. Love yourself by seeking and finding more balance.

Why?—Because joy is limitless. Joy is a perpetual flywheel of positive energy spreading out and arousing everyone it touches.

Create your joy—then leak it unreservedly.

CHAPTER SIX

The Habitudes of Nurturing Vulnerability and Avoiding Judgment

Vulnerability is the source of hope, empathy, accountability, and authenticity. If we want greater clarity in our purpose or deeper and more meaningful spiritual lives, vulnerability is the path." – Brené Brown

Vulnerability: Telling Your Story With Your Whole Heart

When I began *The Power of Heart Language*, I decided at first to focus and write only about five heart language habitudes.

Fortunately, I am blessed to have some wonderfully bright friends and extraordinary colleagues. And, as my book began to take shape, I had many opportunities to discuss the ideas and concepts, the exercises, and to explain (and sometimes defend) my point of view and belief in the 80/20 importance of limiting the book to the five original habitudes.

Not surprisingly, I entertained several "what if" discussions about the possibility of adding one or two more habitudes.

However, I argued gently with myself (and others) that sharing gratitude, embracing forgiveness, fearlessly listening, spreading encouragement, and leaking joy are tangible expressions of emotional vulnerability.

Nevertheless, I agree with my dear friend, Dr. Bruce Stafford, that the willingness to be emotionally vulnerable with another person is one of the most powerful ways to create empathy and deep connection; vulnerability is indeed a loving characteristic of extraordinary relationships.

In her forthcoming book, *Rattle The Cage—How To Shape The Behaviors You Want In Your Pets, Children (And Even Your Spouse)* my friend, and talented therapist Kimberley Walker, offers this unique viewpoint on vulnerability:

> Vulnerability begins in your heart. Diligently work on identifying your 'inner truth' with yourself first. Start by having an authentic conversation about what you value most, beliefs about yourself and your place in the world in order to be vulnerable with others. If you do this, you are assured to connect with others on the deepest level.

In her popular TEDTalk, *The Power of Vulnerability*, (27,000,000+ views) Dr. Brené Brown reported her research findings of people she describes as "wholehearted."

> And so here's what I found. What wholehearted people had in common was a sense of courage. And I want to separate courage and bravery for you for a minute.
>
> Courage, the original definition of courage, when it first came into the English language, was from the Latin word "cor" meaning "heart." And the original definition was to tell the story of who you are with your whole heart. And so these [whole-hearted] folks had, very simply, the courage to be imperfect.

They had the compassion to be kind to themselves first and then to others, because, as it turns out, we can't practice compassion with other people if we can't treat ourselves kindly. And the last was, they had connection—and this was the hard part—as a result of authenticity, they were willing to let go of who they thought they should be in order to be who they were, which you have to absolutely do that for connection.

The other thing that they had in common was this: They fully embraced vulnerability. They believed that what made them vulnerable—made them beautiful. They didn't talk about vulnerability being comfortable, nor did they really talk about it being excruciating. They just talked about it being necessary. They were willing to invest in a relationship that may or may not work out. They thought this was fundamental.

Even after a year or so playing tennis together, I still can't say I had more than a surface-level relationship with one of my partners. I admired his competitive spirit, quick mind, and his on-court skills, but to me, he seemed a bit aloof. (Who knows what he thought of me?)

One afternoon, after finishing our workout, he invited me to visit for a few minutes. He told me his sister had died in a car accident a few days earlier. He began to talk about his grief, about his closeness with his sister, how his mother had passed within weeks of his sister, and how he worried about his father. For almost an hour he was completely and utterly open and vulnerable in a way I hadn't expected. As he continued, I began to realize that this was an authentic, sensitive, person in front of me with endearing qualities that I had somehow overlooked.

We soon began having lunch together on a regular basis. Over the coming months, I looked forward to Larry's "single-guy-internet-dating" stories and self-deprecating sense of humor. We discovered that we enjoyed many of the same books, and shared a deep appreciation for the art and science of sales, marketing, and people-communications.

Now, some ten years later, he is one of my closest friends. I was honored to be the best man for his wedding, and my wife and I have both grown to love his amazing wife Lisa and their remarkable circle of friends.

It was his willingness to be emotionally vulnerable that bridged the gap in our relationship and led to a deep and meaningful friendship.

That experience, in part, leads me to suggest one more habitude worth noting and adopting.

The Habitude of Avoiding Judgment

I've experienced again and again in life where my own premature and "thin sliced" conclusions (looks, clothes, color, language, body type, whatever) have served only to limit my possible connection and closeness with others.

Author, Malcolm Gladwell, explains in his book, "*Blink. The Power of Thinking Without Thinking*", that all humans are hard-wired to make split-second cognitive decisions about the people they meet; especially in situations where they are under stress.

Harvard researchers, Nalini Ambady and Robert Rosenthal, report that most of us have a strong tendency to make rapid judgments about the people we meet—again, thin slices—and unfortunately, we rarely change them.

When it comes to the understanding of our world and ourselves, these immediate impressions and conclusions, especially about others, at times can serve us well—but just as often serve us poorly.

There are countless stories about first responders and life emergencies when instant decisions saved lives. [Flight #1549—The Miracle on the Hudson] Yet, at the same time, there are too many examples where snap decisions combined with anti-social judgments created heartbreaking tragedies. [Trayvon Martin shooting, Sanford Florida, 2012]

I'm almost certain most of us can share a story about people who we've come to know and love deeply—but in the beginning, we completely misjudged.

But to be clear, by developing the habitude of avoiding judgment I mean learning to avoid the nearly instantaneous and unsupported conclusions you make about others—with little more to go on than a haircut, a piece of clothing or a body type. Often we jump to conclusions about the people we meet, and then keep looking for more evidence to support our original conclusion.

Here's an example from of a thought-provoking story about a young man, who appeared to be in his twenties, looking out from a train window:

> "Look, dad," he yells out loudly, "those trees are going fast behind us."
>
> Across the aisle, a passenger frowns, obviously annoyed at the noise level and the young man's immature behavior.
>
> Then he cries out again, "Dad, dad, look! The clouds are running with us!"
>
> Finally, the irritated passenger says to the father, "Perhaps you should consider taking your son to see a good eye doctor."
>
> The boy's father smiled and answered, "Yes, we are just returning from the hospital. My son has been blind from

birth, and today after his third eye operation is the first time he has ever been able to see."

"I'm so sorry he bothered you. He's very excited."

It's challenging to fight our human tendency to judge other people and their situations before we know what's going on. It reminds me of a story Dr. Joel Hunter, shared one Sunday at our church.

A young woman moved to a rural area with her new husband, and soon made friends with her nearby neighbor. The young woman couldn't help but notice that her older friend seemed to be continually busy—always serving her husband and children. One day while the new friends were visiting, the older woman's husband walked up to the porch, nodded hello, and set a large catch of fish on the table and walked away.

The younger woman was astonished to see her older friend get up immediately and begin cleaning the fish.

"I don't understand you," the young woman blurted. "If my husband brought those ugly things to our home, I'd tell him to get busy and clean them himself. I'm sure it's none of my business, but to me, it seems quite rude."

The older woman looked at her friend and smiled. "I was very sick and lay in bed for almost two years. My husband took good care of me. He watched our four children. He changed my bedpan every day. He worked two jobs to pay for my medicine. He read to me every night when I couldn't sleep. And, when I began feeling well again, he bought me a new washer and dryer so I wouldn't have to clean the clothes by hand."

He never once complained—not ever! I hope you can understand ... I gladly clean his fish."

Our deep-rooted human tendencies to judge others without real evidence are here to stay. But, I'm optimistic that

140

what we *can do* is continue to remind ourselves to "fight off" and then release our petty judgments of others and strive to replace them with habitudes that create compassion, discernment, empathy, and understanding.

What if each of us replaced our habits of gossip and judgment with the habits of speaking only good things about other people and by example, encouraged others to do the same? What kind of positive energy, love, healing, miracles, and joy could we create?

It's important to know that discernment is distinct from judgment. If it's clear that a person or relationship demoralizes you, prevents you from growing, endangers your dignity—and you have done everything you can to prevent its failure—then it's time to walk away.

Always walk away from any relationship that makes you feel small and insecure and instead seek out those who inspire, support, and encourage you. The ultimate measure of any great relationship is in how much it supports and encourages your (and the other person's) intellectual, emotional, and spiritual growth.

Thank You—I Appreciate You!

My goal was to offer proven tools to help you create extraordinary relationships in your life. I am so grateful—so honored—that you took the time to read this book

I believe from the very moment you (and I) commit to communicating with the languages of the heart, we will begin to create extraordinary connections with others—and begin attracting miracles into our lives.

And after all, if we're not busy attracting miracles, what's the point anyway?

How to Keep Improving Your Heart Language Skills

If you'd like to learn more, need additional information, have any thoughts, questions, comments, a recommendation or even a story you'd like to share, please feel free to contact me through my website:

www.montetaylor.com/heartlanguage

I wish you tremendous joy and success in your life's journey

Monte Taylor, Jr.

INDEX

Made in the USA
Columbia, SC
01 June 2019